# ENTRÉES
# FROM YOUR BREAD MACHINE

## Donna Rathmell German

**BRISTOL PUBLISHING ENTERPRISES**
San Leandro, California

# a nitty gritty® cookbook

Printed in the United States of America.
ISBN 1-55867-145-5

Cover design: Frank J. Paredes
Cover photography: John A. Benson
Food stylist: Merilee Hague Bordin
Illustrator: Mike Nelson

# CONTENTS

No book could be written without the support
of friends and family, for which I am very grateful.

Many thanks to Kathy Atkinson, Karen Gilbert, Josi Hunt,
Libby O'Brien and Pam Schrieber for sharing ideas, tasting, testing
and general moral support.

Thanks also to the numerous tasters, who ate many
different breads and meals.

As always, thanks to my three daughters, Rachel, Katie and Helen,
who are becoming quite good bakers themselves, and who don't hesitate
to critique! My husband provided moral support through letters from sea.

# ABOUT BREAD MACHINES AND BREADS

Almost everyone with a bread machine is looking for more ways to use this favored appliance. This book will give you ideas and recipes for using your bread machine to produce the main dish or "the main event" for every meal of the day, as well as for snack time or party time. A collection of desserts is included.

Every effort has been made to develop a wide range of recipes, but I must admit that in some cases I was nearly carried away with a theme. I had never tasted a bread salad before I began work on this book but, as the saying goes, it was love at first bite. I could have added many more bread salads. The same is true of other categories, such as focaccia, or crostini, or turnover-style sandwiches, or bread bowls with dips, or flavored yeast cakes. You are encouraged to use these recipes as a basis for your own experimentation.

Time and convenience are important, and I have included many recipes that can be totally or partially prepared in advance, such as breakfast breads and coffee cakes, bread puddings, stratas and some of the desserts.

Many recipes call for dough made on the *dough* or *manual* cycle of your bread machine. Other recipes call for slices of flavored breads made in the bread machine in the normal fashion, usually enough to make approximately 4 to 6 servings. The *Essential Breads for Entrées* were specifically developed for recipes on the following pages, but each can also be enjoyed on its own.

Keep bags of leftover bread slices in your freezer, marked sweet, herb, etc., and use them whenever you need bread for these recipes or others. Breads with complimentary flavors can often be combined.

Many of the recipes call for a given number of slices of bread. Most loaves have a width of 5 to 6 inches. A slice of bread about ½-inch thick will range in weight (depending on ingredients) from 1¼ to 1¾ oz. Most of the recipes are not dependent on the size or weight of the slices but, if they are, I give an alternative way of measuring, such as "2 slices bread or 2 cups bread cubes."

## GENERAL BREAD AND DOUGH-MAKING DIRECTIONS

There are a few pieces of information that you must determine about your particular machine in order to know how to make any recipe. Specific information about your machine can be found in your owner's manual or the recipe booklet that came with the machine.

### Ingredient Order

Manufacturers indicate the order in which the ingredients should be put into the pan. In 9 out of 10 machines, you start with the liquid; in the other 10%, you begin with yeast and then flour. For example, many DAK, Welbilt and Citizen machines call for yeast and flour first, so the liquid will not leak through the hole in the bottom of the pan. For such machines, reverse the order of ingredients in my recipes, beginning with yeast. *The really important point is that the liquid ingredients are kept away from the yeast until the machine starts.*

## Recipe Size For Your Machine

You must first determine the size of your machine. Machines are sold as 1 lb., 1½ lb. or 2 lb. machines. This may be somewhat confusing, because the weight of a loaf will vary depending on the ingredients used. If your machine manual does not specify the size of the machine given by weight of loaf, it is easily determined by looking at the amount of flour in the recipes that come with the machine.

In general, **1 lb. machines** use 2 to 2¼ cups of bread flour or 2 to 2¾ total cups of combined flours such as bread flour with whole wheat, rye, oats, corn, etc.

A 1½ **lb. machine** uses 3 cups of bread flour or 3½ to 4 total cups of combined flours such as bread flour with whole wheat, rye, oats, corn, etc. Up to 5 cups of whole grain flours can be used in most 1½ lb. machines without fear of overflows.

A full **2 lb. machine** can use up to 4 cups of bread flour, although I find that 3½ cups usually results in a nice loaf of bread at or just over the lip of the pan. A total of

4 to 5 cups of combined flours such as bread flour, whole wheat, oats, rye, corn, etc. can easily be used, and up to 6 cups of whole grain flours.

Some machines are being sold as 2 lb. machines, but the size of the pan is the same as the 1½ lb. pan, and therefore, must generally use the 1½ lb. size of my recipes.

After years of working with all machine makes and models, I can assure you that there are some variables and individual preferences in the sizes of recipes used. For example, one friend with a 1 lb. machine (2 cups of flour generally) makes 1½ lb. recipes, which would seem too large for her machine. My father, however, has a large machine and consistently uses recipes with just 2 cups of flour; in the identical machine I use 3½ cups of flour with success.

Unlike any other bread machine cookbook on the market, I give you three different sizes for each recipe. If the recipe is too large, next time use a smaller size. With the exception of National/Panasonic 65 model machines, all machines can make a smaller size recipe.

## Choosing a Cycle

Usually a sweet cycle (which may or may not be your raisin cycle) has a lower baking temperature and perhaps a longer rising time. If the recipe calls for a sweet or basic cycle, use a sweet cycle if you have one. If your machine has a raisin cycle but no specific sweet cycle, use the raisin cycle. If you don't have either, then use the basic cycle. You may want to use a light crust setting if your machine has a color selector.

In general, use the first cycle listed in the recipe if you have it; if not, go to the next cycle until you find one that you have.

**Adding Raisins or Other Ingredients Indicated With an Asterisk (\*)**

A raisin cycle may be called *raisin, sweet, mix,* or *fruit and nut,* or there may not be such a cycle on your machine. There may be a "beep" for adding raisins about 5 minutes before the end of the last kneading. Some machines do not have a beep, or you may find that the raisins or other additional ingredients are best added earlier in the kneading to achieve better distribution. The majority of machines have two full kneadings with a 15- to 25-minute rest in between. If this is the case, you can add the raisins at the beginning of the second kneading. I sometimes put the additional ingredients on top of the dough during the rest stage, where they sit waiting for the kneading, so I don't forget. If your machine has only one full kneading of 15 to 20 minutes, you should add the additional ingredients about 10 minutes into the kneading.

# BREAD MAKING HINTS

Perhaps the single most important thing to check is the consistency of the dough after 5 to 10 minutes of kneading. With few exceptions, the dough should form a nice, smooth ball. Sometimes the ball will be round and other times, it may take on more of a cylindrical shape which "tornadoes" up the side of the pan. The dough should feel moist but not really sticky. Dough that is too dry will not mix properly or it may cause the machine to struggle (you'll hear it). It may be uneven or have two or more balls of dough. If this is the case, simply add whatever liquid you are using, one tablespoon at a time, until the required consistency is obtained. Conversely, dough that is too wet will not form a ball, and flour should be added a tablespoon at a time until the required consistency is obtained.

Warm the liquid (microwave for 30 to 60 seconds) so that it feels warm on the inside of your wrist, about 110°.

Butter or margarine does not need to be melted. Measure and cut it into smaller pieces or quarters. Oils and other fats can be substituted on a tablespoon-for-tablespoon basis. Fat substitutes such as applesauce or thawed frozen apple, grape and orange juice concentrates can also be used on a tablespoon-for-tablespoon basis.

Eggs can be used either straight from the refrigerator or at room temperature.

Bread flour is higher in protein than all-purpose flour and is best for recipes baked in the bread machine. Some recipes made on the dough cycle use all-purpose flour, which is a combination of a high protein bread flour and a soft pastry flour, for a lighter texture.

The yeast used in testing was instant, fast rising or quick rising, which is also sold under the name *bread machine yeast*. Active dry yeast can be used, but the amounts given in the recipes should be heaped.

## USING THE DOUGH CYCLE

Most machines have a separate *dough* or *manual* cycle that kneads the dough, lets the dough rise in the machine and turns the machine off, at which point you remove the dough. A very few machines beep to tell you that the first rise is complete. If you have such a machine, remove the dough at the end of the first rise and turn off the machine. The dough is shaped according to the recipe directions, perhaps allowed to rise again and then baked in a conventional oven. Dough/manual cycles range in time from 50 minutes to 1 hour and 40 minutes. With the exception of the Citizen, DAK and Welbilt ABM 100 machines, all recipes were tested using the full dough cycle. These machines, however, have a 1-hour rise after the initial kneading and then a second kneading of 20 to 30 minutes. I find the dough difficult to work after this long second kneading, and prefer to stop the machine and remove the dough after it has risen for an hour.

All machines are capable of kneading up to 4 cups of flour, even a 1 lb. machine. Please do not try to bake dough cycle recipes in your machine. If you have a 1 lb. machine and the dough is rising too high, you can either puncture the dough to deflate it and allow it to continue with the cycle, or you can remove the dough and shape it then, as the cycle is probably only a few minutes from completion.

Unless otherwise specified, lightly flour your hands to prevent sticking when you remove the dough from the machine. The work surface should be very lightly floured, but do not use too much flour, as it may cause the final product to become tough and chewy.

When dividing dough into a given number of equal pieces, first roll the dough into a log. Divide the log in half and then each half in half (quarters). Divide each quarter into the appropriate number.

If at any time during rolling or shaping the dough becomes difficult to work, let it rest for 5 to 10 minutes. The gluten will relax and it will be easier to shape.

Butter all baking pans, spray them with nonstick vegetable spray or line them with parchment paper.

To double a dough recipe, make one batch of dough in the machine and allow it to knead completely. Remove the dough after the kneading is complete (10 to 15 minutes) and place it in a large, greased bowl. Cover with a towel and place in a warm, draft-free location to rise. Make the second batch of dough on the dough/manual cycle. When the cycle is complete, both batches of dough are ready to be used.

## INGREDIENTS

Always use the best quality, freshest ingredients you can find.

Testing has indicated that the best yeast for bread machine baking is fast acting yeast, also called quick rise, rapid rise or bread machine yeast. (See note, page 7.)

Several recipes call for lemon or orange peel, which is available in dried form in the grocery store spice section. Fresh peel from a lemon or orange can be substituted on a teaspoon-for-teaspoon basis, using a simple zester found in any kitchen shop. Because it is difficult to remove zest from the fruit into a measuring spoon, I generally remove it from the fruit directly into the bread machine pan to my taste.

If lemon juice is called for, you can use fresh lemon juice or commercially bottled lemon juice. An easy way to juice a lemon is to roll it on the counter while pressing down with the palm of your hand. You'll feel the lemon start to soften and it will be easier to juice.

Garlic is best when it is freshly minced or chopped. However, minced or chopped garlic is available in jars in the produce section of the grocery store, and is very convenient; ½ tsp. minced garlic equals about 1 clove.

Like garlic, ginger is best freshly chopped, but chopped ginger can also be found in jars in the produce section. I prefer it to either chopping my own or, by far, to the dried, ground ginger in the spice section, which is not as flavorful. a 1-x-½-inch piece of peeled ginger root makes about 1 tsp. chopped ginger root and is roughly equivalent to ¼ tsp. ground ginger.

I use a child's "sippy" cup with a plastic lid and a hole for drinking to melt butter in the microwave. The hole allows steam to vent, but the lid prevents the butter or margarine from splattering. These cups are inexpensive and easily found in the baby food section of the grocery store.

Several recipes call for leftover meats, usually chicken. If you do not have leftovers, ½ lb. deli turkey equals approximately 1½ cups diced meat. Four boneless chicken breast halves, diced and sautéed in a little olive oil, grilled or microwaved, will give you about 2 cups cooked chicken.

## LEFTOVER BREAD

After you have fed the ducks and birds, just what can you do with all the leftovers?

Recipes in this book which can use leftover breads are indicated. As long as the leftover breads complement each other, several different types of breads can be combined in the recipes. For example, if you have slices of an herb bread, onion bread and plain bread, you can combine all three in a bread salad or in any recipe using an herb-flavored bread. The flavors of the breads come through and dress up an ordinary recipe.

Slices of leftover bread can be stored in the freezer in locking freezer bags. Provide separate bags for sweet breads, herb breads, spicy breads, plain breads, etc. If you want toast with breakfast or dinner, you can simply remove one or two slices and toast them. When you have enough leftovers or the mood strikes, you can choose from the many recipes in this book!

Leftover bread can also be dried. Dried herb breads make wonderful crumbs or croutons for casseroles, salads or other recipes. Dried sweet breads made with butter instead of olive oil make interesting crumb toppings or crisp sweet crackers to accompany ice cream or yogurt. To dry bread, spray or brush slices of leftover bread with water, olive oil or melted butter, place them on a lightly greased or sprayed baking sheet or perforated pizza pan and bake in a warm (200°) oven for 1½ to 2 hours until dry and crisp. You can turn the bread over after an hour or so if you wish. Thinly sliced bread will dry quicker and can be used as crackers, while thicker slices of bread can be processed with a food processor quickly for large chunks (croutons) or longer for crumbs. Use them within a day or two if fat was added. Otherwise, store croutons or crumbs in a tin container or a brown paper bag until ready to use. I have had bread crackers last in a brown paper bag for up to two months. For a little extra flavor, an herb or plain bread can be rubbed with a cut clove of garlic before toasting.

Add pieces of fresh, stale or dried bread to a hearty soup to thicken it or as a substitute for oyster crackers. Onion soup doesn't seem right if it is served without chunks of bread in it — try leftover flavorful herb or onion bread instead of a basic French bread. Tomato soup becomes more elegant when you layer the bottom of the soup bowl with bite-sized pieces of leftover onion bread before you fill the bowl with soup.

Rub a thick slice of leftover herb or plain bread with a piece of cut garlic and brush with a little olive oil. Toast in a 300° oven for about 30 minutes or on the grill for 5 minutes or until it starts to dry.

# ESSENTIAL BREADS FOR ENTRÉES

# KIDS' WHITE BREAD

Sweet, Basic Cycle; no timer

*Children who love that soft, squishy bread will love this! As soon as it is removed from the machine, wrap the warm bread in a cloth kitchen towel and then wrap it in plastic to help keep the crust soft. For some real fun, add food coloring (¼ tsp. for vibrant colors) to coordinate with any holiday, red for Christmas or Valentine's Day, yellow for spring or any time of the year, orange for Halloween. Green is a bit unappetizing, so avoid that one! Set crust color to light.*

|                    | 1 lb.      | 1½ lb.   | 1¾ lb.     |
|--------------------|------------|----------|------------|
| milk               | ⅔ cup      | 1 cup    | 1⅛ cups    |
| egg                | 1          | 1        | 1          |
| butter or margarine| 1 tbs.     | 2 tbs.   | 2 tbs.     |
| sugar              | 2 tbs.     | 3 tbs.   | ¼ cup      |
| salt               | ½ tsp.     | ¾ tsp.   | 1 tsp.     |
| bread flour        | 2 cups     | 3 cups   | 3½ cups    |
| yeast              | 1½ tsp.    | 2 tsp.   | 2 tsp.     |

**See *Welsh Rarebit for Kids*, page 92**     **use in any recipe as a plain leftover bread**

# FRUIT BREAD

*The cinnamon can easily be adjusted to taste, even doubled. While raisins are the most commonly used dried fruit in breads, try dried peaches, cranberries, blueberries or cherries, etc. For a stronger flavor and a denser (lower rising) loaf, double the amount of dried fruit. Set crust color to light or medium.*

|  | 1 lb. | 1½ lb. | 1¾ lb. |
|---|---|---|---|
| water | ¾ cup | 1¼ cups | 1⅓ cups |
| butter or margarine | 1 tbs. | 1½ tbs. | 2 tbs. |
| sugar | 2 tbs. | 2½ tbs. | 3 tbs. |
| salt | ½ tsp. | ¾ tsp. | 1 tsp. |
| cinnamon | 1 tsp. | 1½ tsp. | 2 tsp. |
| bread flour | 2 cups | 3 cups | 3½ cups |
| yeast | 1½ tsp. | 2 tsp. | 2 tsp. |
| *raisins or other dried fruit | ¼ cup | ⅓ cup | ⅓ cup |
| *chopped or sliced nuts | ⅓ cup | ½ cup | ⅔ cup |

*Add ingredients at the beep; see page 5.

**See *Roast Chicken with Cranberry Stuffing*, page 138**

**See *Traditional Bread Pudding*, page 145**
**See *Colonial American Fruit Dessert*, page 166**

# LEMON BREAD

*Make this bread with freshly squeezed or bottled lemon juice. Fresh lemon peel (zest) can be stripped directly into the bread pan to taste, or use the amounts given in the recipe for dried peel. Set crust color to light or medium.*

|  | 1 lb. | 1½ lb. | 1¾ lb. |
|---|---|---|---|
| water | ⅔ cup | 1 cup | 1⅛ cups |
| lemon juice | 2 tbs. | 2½ tbs. | 3 tbs. |
| butter | 1 tbs. | 1 tbs. | 2 tbs. |
| sugar | 2 tbs. | 3 tbs. | ¼ cup |
| salt | ½ tsp. | ¾ tsp. | 1 tsp. |
| lemon peel | 1 tsp. | 1½ tsp. | 2 tsp. |
| bread flour | 2 cups | 3 cups | 3½ cups |
| yeast | 1 tsp. | 1½ tsp. | 1½ tsp. |

See *Spanish Fried Bread*, page 71
See *Spanish Toast*, page 73
See *Austrian Egg Cake*, page 104
See *Traditional Bread Pudding*, page 145
See *Tropical Bread Pudding*, page 146

See *Piña Colada Bread Pudding*, page 147
See *Mexican Capriotada*, page 148
See *Peach Betty*, page 150
See *Lemon Layered Cake*, page 156
See *Colonial American Fruit Dessert*, page 166

# ORANGE BREAD

Sweet, Raisin or Basic Cycle

*I use commercially prepared orange juice sold in cartons, not orange juice from frozen concentrate. Spread leftover slices with butter, sprinkle with a little orange peel, dry in a 200° oven for 1½ to 2 hours and serve as a crisp sweet cracker with orange sherbet. Set crust color to light or medium.*

|  | 1 lb. | 1½ lb. | 1¾ lb. |
|---|---|---|---|
| orange juice | ⅔ cup | 1 cup | 1¼ cups |
| egg | 1 | 1 | 1 |
| butter | 1 tbs. | 1 tbs. | 2 tbs. |
| sugar | 1 tbs. | 1½ tbs. | 2 tbs. |
| salt | ½ tsp. | ¾ tsp. | 1 tsp. |
| orange peel | 1½ tsp. | 2 tsp. | 1 tbs. |
| bread flour | 2 cups | 3 cups | 3½ cups |
| yeast | 1 tsp. | 1½ tsp. | 1½ tsp. |

See *Strawberry Breakfast Pudding*, page 70
See *Spanish Toast Bites*, page 72
See *Spanish Toast*, page 73
See *Austrian Egg Cake*, page 104
See *Dutch Egg Cake*, page 105

See *Traditional Bread Pudding*, page 145
See *Tropical Bread Pudding*, page 146
See *Mexican Capriotada*, page 148
See *Strawberry Pudding*, page 149
See *Colonial American Fruit Dessert*, page 166

# HAWAIIAN BREAD

*This bread is one of those "most requested" recipes. Although the bread is sweet, it makes terrific ham or turkey sandwiches. You can also serve it toasted with butter as a side to the ham. Set crust color to light or medium.*

|  | **1 lb.** | **1½ lb.** | **1¾ lb.** |
|---|---|---|---|
| pineapple juice | ⅔ cup | 1 cup | 1⅛ cups |
| egg | 1 | 1 | 1 |
| butter or margarine | 1 tbs. | 2 tbs. | 3 tbs. |
| sugar | 2 tbs. | 3 tbs. | ¼ cup |
| salt | ¾ tsp. | 1 tsp. | 1 tsp. |
| bread flour | 2 cups | 3 cups | 3½ cups |
| yeast | 1½ tsp. | 2 tsp. | 2 tsp. |

**See *Hawaiian Toast*, page 76**
**See *Ham and Cheese Strata*, page 99**
**See *Austrian Egg Cake*, page 104**

**See *Tropical Bread Pudding*, page 146**
**See *Piña Colada Bread Pudding*, page 147**

# APRICOT BREAD

*There is no sugar in this recipe, as the apricots and the nectar contain enough to raise the bread. If you don't want to make French toast, this makes wonderful plain toast, too. It is also a wonderful accompaniment to a pork dinner if toasted in the oven or on the grill with a little butter (with or without a little ginger) — garlic bread-style. Set crust color to light or medium.*

|                        | **1 lb.**  | **1½ lb.**  | **1¾ lb.**  |
|------------------------|------------|-------------|-------------|
| apricot nectar         | ⅞ cup      | 1¼ cups     | 1½ cups     |
| butter                 | 1 tbs.     | 1 tbs.      | 2 tbs.      |
| salt                   | ½ tsp.     | ¾ tsp.      | 1 tsp.      |
| bread flour            | 2 cups     | 3 cups      | 3½ cups     |
| yeast                  | 1 tsp.     | 1½ tsp.     | 1½ tsp.     |
| *chopped dried apricots | ½ cup     | ⅔ cup       | ¾ cup       |

*Add ingredients at the beep; see page 5.

See *French Toast Cajun-Style*, page 75
See *Pork Tenderloin With Apricot Stuffing*, page 137

See *Peach Betty*, page 150

ESSENTIAL BREADS FOR ENTRÉES 19

# COCONUT BREAD

*Chopped macadamia nuts can be substituted for the almonds for a real tropical flavor. Spread leftover slices with butter, sprinkle with a little orange or lemon peel, dry in a 200° oven for 1½ to 2 hours and serve as a crisp sweet cracker with orange or lemon sherbet. Set crust color to light or medium.*

|  | **1 lb.** | **1½ lb.** | **1¾ lb.** |
| --- | --- | --- | --- |
| milk | ⅔ cup | 1⅛ cups | 1⅓ cups |
| butter | 2 tbs. | 3 tbs. | 3 tbs. |
| coconut extract | 1 tsp. | 1½ tsp. | 2 tsp. |
| sugar | 2 tbs. | 3 tbs. | ¼ cup |
| salt | ½ tsp. | ¾ tsp. | 1 tsp. |
| coconut flakes | ½ cup | ⅔ cup | ¾ cup |
| bread flour | 2 cups | 3 cups | 3½ cups |
| yeast | 1½ tsp. | 2 tsp. | 2 tsp. |
| *sliced almonds | ⅓ cup | ½ cup | ⅔ cup |

*Add ingredients at the beep; see page 5.

See *Ginger Shrimp Crostini*, page 334
See *Strawberry Breakfast Pudding*, page 70
See *Walnut French Toast*, page 74
See *Hawaiian Toast*, page 76

See *Piña Colada Bread Pudding*, page 147
See *Strawberry Pudding*, page 149
See *Layered Chocolate Coconut Cake*, page 154

# APPLE CINNAMON RAISIN BREAD

Raisin, Sweet or Basic Cycle

*Enjoy this bread toasted for breakfast or a mid-afternoon snack. Chopped dried apples can be substituted for the raisins. Set crust color to light or medium.*

| | 1 lb. | 1½ lb. | 1¾ lb. |
|---|---|---|---|
| apple juice | ⅔ cup | 1⅛ cups | 1¼ cups |
| vegetable oil | 1 tbs. | 1½ tbs. | 2 tbs. |
| honey or maple syrup | 1 tbs. | 1½ tbs. | 2 tbs. |
| salt | ½ tsp. | ¾ tsp. | 1 tsp. |
| cinnamon | 1 tsp. | 1½ tsp. | 2 tsp. |
| oats | ½ cup | ⅔ cup | ¾ cup |
| bread flour | 2 cups | 3 cups | 3½ cups |
| yeast | 1½ tsp. | 2 tsp. | 2 tsp. |
| *raisins | ¼ cup | ⅓ cup | ½ cup |
| *chopped walnuts, optional | ¼ cup | ⅓ cup | ½ cup |

*Add ingredients at the beep; see page 5.

See *Roast Chicken with Cranberry Stuffing*, page 138
See *Traditional Bread Pudding*, page 145

See *Apple Raisin Betty*, page 151
See *Apple Charlotte*, page 152
See *Easy Cream Layered Cake*, page 153

# CRANBERRY NUT BREAD

Raisin, Sweet or Basic Cycle

*I like walnuts in this bread, but pecans or almonds will work. Fresh orange peel (zest) can be used instead of the dry peel. Strip zest directly into the bread machine pan to taste. Good any time of year, it's especially good in the fall — what a decadent bread for leftover turkey sandwiches! Set crust color to light or medium.*

|  | 1 lb. | 1½ lb. | 1¾ lb. |
|---|---|---|---|
| cranberry juice | ⅞ cup | 1⅛ cups | 1⅓ cups |
| butter | 2 tbs. | 3 tbs. | 3 tbs. |
| sugar | 2 tbs. | 3 tbs. | ¼ cup |
| salt | ¼ tsp. | ½ tsp. | ¾ tsp. |
| orange peel | 1 tsp. | 1½ tsp. | 2 tsp. |
| bread flour | 2 cups | 3 cups | 3½ cups |
| yeast | 1½ tsp. | 2 tsp. | 2 tsp. |
| *chopped walnuts | ⅓ cup | ½ cup | ⅔ cup |
| *craisins or raisins | ¼ cup | ⅓ cup | ½ cup |

*Add ingredients at the beep; see page 5.

See *Turkey Strata*, page 98
See *Roast Chicken With Cranberry Stuffing*,
   page 138

See *Easy Cream Layered Cake*, page 153
See *Traditional Bread Pudding*, page 145

# FRENCH WALNUT BREAD

Raisin, Sweet or Basic Cycle

*The walnut oil really adds flavor and is found in some larger grocery stores. If you can't find it, use vegetable or canola oil. Enjoy this bread fresh, or dried like crostini, with Brie cheese and some wine. Or serve a very thick slice with soup for lunch. Set crust color to light or medium.*

|  | **1 lb.** | **1½ lb.** | **1¾ lb.** |
|---|---|---|---|
| water | ¾ cup | 1 cup | 1⅛ cups |
| walnut oil | 2 tbs. | 3 tbs. | ¼ cup |
| sugar | 3 tbs. | ¼ cup | ¼ cup |
| salt | ¾ tsp. | 1 tsp. | 1 tsp. |
| bread flour | 2 cups | 3 cups | 3½ cups |
| yeast | 1 tsp. | 1½ tsp. | 1½ tsp. |
| *chopped walnuts | ½ cup | ⅔ cup | ¾ cup |

*Add ingredients at the beep; see page 5.

See *Strawberry Breakfast Pudding*, page 70
See *Walnut French Toast*, page 74

See *Easy Cream Layered Cake*, page 153

# CARAWAY BREAD

*Any whole aromatic seed can be used in lieu of the caraway to complement any meal being served. Try anise, celery, coriander, cumin, dill, fennel, flax, mustard, poppy or sesame seeds. Or substitute small whole grains such as amaranth or quinoa to add flavor, nutrition and crunch. Set crust color to medium.*

|                      | 1 lb.      | 1½ lb.     | 1¾ lb.     |
|----------------------|------------|------------|------------|
| water                | ⅞ cup      | 1⅛ cups    | 1⅓ cups    |
| butter or margarine  | 1 tbs.     | 1 tbs.     | 1½ tbs.    |
| sugar                | 1 tbs.     | 1½ tbs.    | 2 tbs.     |
| salt                 | ½ tsp.     | ¾ tsp.     | 1 tsp.     |
| caraway seeds        | 1 tbs.     | 1½ tbs.    | 2 tbs.     |
| bread flour          | 2 cups     | 3 cups     | 3½ cups    |
| yeast                | 1 tsp.     | 1½ tsp.    | 1½ tsp.    |

See *Crab Crostini*, page 34
See *Broccoli and Cheese Strata*, page 100
See *Creole Bread Pudding*, page 102

See *Swedish Bread Casserole*, page 115
See *Roast Chicken With Sausage Stuffing*, page 138

# RYE BREAD

*The cocoa powder gives the bread a darker color and can be considered optional if you want a light color, or if you don't have any on hand. For variety, replace the caraway with fennel, or simply omit it. Rye does not have much gluten and is generally low rising or requires very long rising times. This recipe contains enough rye flour to flavor the bread, but not too much to affect the rising. Set crust color to medium.*

|  | **1 lb.** | **1½ lb.** | **1¾ lb.** |
|---|---|---|---|
| water | 1 cup | 1⅓ cups | 1⅔ cups |
| vegetable oil | 1 tbs. | 1 tbs. | 1½ tbs. |
| honey | 1½ tbs. | 2 tbs. | 3 tbs. |
| salt | ½ tsp. | ½ tsp. | 1 tsp. |
| unsweetened cocoa powder | 1 tbs. | 1½ tbs. | 2 tbs. |
| caraway seeds | 1 tbs. | 1½ tbs. | 2 tbs. |
| rye flour | ⅔ cup | ¾ cup | 1 cup |
| bread flour | 2 cups | 2½ cups | 3 cups |
| yeast | 1½ tsp. | 2 tsp. | 2 tsp. |

See *Crab Crostini*, page 35                    See *Swedish Bread Casserole*, page 115
See *Cheese Fondues*, page 50

# ONION BREAD

Basic Cycle; timer

*The onions should be freshly chopped so they are nice and juicy. As always, however, watch the dough, as the liquid from the onions could affect the consistency. Add water or flour if necessary. Dried pieces of this bread make wonderful crackers or nibbles, and the fresh bread makes terrific sandwiches of just about any variety — if you like onions, of course! Set crust color to medium.*

|  | **1 lb.** | **1½ lb.** | **1¾ lb.** |
|---|---|---|---|
| water | ⅔ cup | 1 cup | 1⅛ cups |
| olive oil | 1 tbs. | 1½ tbs. | 2 tbs. |
| chopped onions | ¼ cup | ⅓ cup | ½ cup |
| sugar | 1 tbs. | 1½ tbs. | 2 tbs. |
| salt | ½ tsp. | ¾ tsp. | 1 tsp. |
| bread flour | 2 cups | 3 cups | 3½ cups |
| yeast | 1 tsp. | 1½ tsp. | 1½ tsp. |

See *Crab Crostini*, page 37
See *Cheese Fondues*, page 50
See *Caribbean Bread Salad*, page 80

See *Crab Strata*, page 101
See *Creole Bread Pudding*, page 102

# SPICY CHEESE CORNMEAL BREAD

Raisin, Sweet or Basic Cycle

*The diced jalapeños (or any favorite hot pepper) can be adjusted to taste. Keep an eye on the dough and adjust as necessary, even after adding the cheese. Serve with chili on a cold evening. Set crust color to light or medium.*

|  | 1 lb. | 1½ lb. | 1¾ lb. |
|---|---|---|---|
| water | 1 cup | 1¼ cups | 1½ cups |
| diced jalapeño peppers | 1 tsp. | 1½ tsp. | 2 tsp. |
| butter or margarine | 1 tbs. | 1½ tbs. | 2 tbs. |
| sugar | 1 tbs. | 1½ tbs. | 2 tbs. |
| salt | ½ tsp. | ¾ tsp. | 1 tsp. |
| cornmeal | ⅓ cup | ½ cup | ¾ cup |
| bread flour | 2 cups | 3 cups | 3½ cups |
| yeast | 1 tsp. | 1½ tsp. | 1½ tsp. |
| *grated cheddar cheese | ¼ cup | ⅓ cup | ½ cup |

*Add ingredients at the beep; see page 5.

See *Mexican Crostini*, page 38
See *Cheese Fondues*, page 50

See *Mexican Bread Salad*, page 81
See *Mexican Bread Pudding*, page 103

# GARLIC BASIL BREAD

Basic Cycle; no timer

*The basil can be adjusted to taste. Load it up for lots of flavor. Use freshly grated Parmesan cheese. This makes great sandwiches — plain tomato is great, but make a BLT with cheese and you'll be in heaven. As a side for dinner, brush bread with olive oil or butter and toast it in the oven or on the grill — mm! Set crust color to medium.*

| | **1 lb.** | **1½ lb.** | **1¾ lb.** |
|---|---|---|---|
| water | ¾ cup | 1⅛ cups | 1¼ cups |
| olive oil | 1 tbs. | 1½ tbs. | 2 tbs. |
| grated Parmesan cheese | 2 tbs. | 3 tbs. | ¼ cup |
| minced garlic | 1 tsp. | 1½ tsp. | 2 tsp. |
| sugar | 1 tbs. | 1½ tbs. | 2 tbs. |
| salt | ½ tsp. | ¾ tsp. | 1 tsp. |
| chopped fresh basil | 4 leaves | 5 leaves | 6 leaves |
|   or dried basil | 1½ tsp. | 2 tsp. | 1 tbs. |
| bread flour | 2 cups | 3 cups | 3½ cups |
| yeast | 1 tsp. | 1½ tsp. | 1½ tsp. |

See *Tomato Basil Crostini*, page 33
See *Cheese Fondues*, page 50
See *Italian Bread Salad*, page 78

See *Meat Loaf in Brioche*, page 132
See *Herbed-Stuffed Chicken Breasts*, page 140
See *Herb-Stuffed Beef Tenderloin*, page 141

# GARLIC PARSLEY BREAD

*This is a delightful bread by itself or as the basis for any number of meals. Use either fresh or dried parsley. Minced garlic in jars, from the grocers' produce section, is convenient. One teaspoon equals 2 cloves minced garlic. Set crust color to medium.*

|  | **1 lb.** | **1½ lb.** | **1¾ lb.** |
|---|---|---|---|
| water | ¾ cup | 1⅛ cups | 1¼ cups |
| olive oil | 2 tbs. | 2½ tbs. | 3 tbs. |
| garlic | 1 tsp. | 1½ tsp. | 2 tsp. |
| sugar | 1 tbs. | 1½ tbs. | 2 tbs. |
| salt | ½ tsp. | ¾ tsp. | 1 tsp. |
| coarsely ground black pepper | ½ tsp. | ¾ tsp. | 1 tsp. |
| chopped fresh parsley | ¼ cup | ⅓ cup | ½ cup |
| bread flour | 2 cups | 3 cups | 3½ cups |
| yeast | 1 tsp. | 1½ tsp. | 1½ tsp. |

See *Cheese Fondues*, page 50
See *Greek Bread Salad*, page 79
See *Crab Strata*, page 101

See *Herbed-Stuffed Chicken Breasts*, page 140
See *Herbed-Stuffed Beef Tenderloin*, page 141
See *Meat Loaf in Brioche*, page 132

ESSENTIAL BREADS FOR ENTRÉES   29

# TOMATO BASIL BREAD

Basic Cycle; timer

*The combination of tomato and basil is as basic as it gets. This version of a tomato basil bread uses canned tomato juice for real ease. As a side for dinner, brush with olive oil or butter and toast in the oven (with or without a little Monterey Jack cheese) or on the grill — mm! Set crust color to medium.*

|  | **1 lb.** | **1½ lb.** | **1¾ lb.** |
|---|---|---|---|
| tomato juice | 1 cup | 1 cups | 1½ cups |
| olive oil | 1½ tbs. | 2 tbs. | 2½ tbs. |
| sugar | 1 tbs. | 1½ tbs. | 2 tbs. |
| salt | ½ tsp. | ¾ tsp. | 1 tsp. |
| chopped fresh basil | 3 tbs. | ¼ cup | ⅓ cup |
|   or dried basil | 1 tbs. | 1½ tbs. | 2 tbs. |
| bread flour | 2 cups | 3 cups | 3½ cups |
| yeast | 1½ tsp. | 2 tsp. | 2 tsp. |

**See *Tomato Basil Crostini*, page 36**          **See *Italian Bread Salad*, page 78**

# APPETIZERS FROM YOUR BREAD MACHINE

# CROSTINI

*Traditionally Italian, crostini are made from leftover Italian bread which has been sautéed or toasted with a little olive oil or butter. The toast is topped with tomatoes and herbs and served warm. Use these directions to make savory Italian-style toasts with traditional or innovative toppings. In addition to these combinations, experiment with any of your favorite breads, and top with other foods, such as pesto, olives, cherry or Roma tomato slices, proscuitto or other favorite hams, olive oil with garlic or ginger, or any favorite cheese and herb. You can prepare crostini in advance and keep them in the refrigerator. Just before serving, pop them into the oven and serve warm.*

Cut slices of bread into quarters (remove crusts if desired) and brush or spray each piece with olive oil. Place on a greased baking sheet or a perforated pizza pan and bake in a 200° oven for 1½ to 2 hours until dry and crisp. Make topping according to recipe directions. Top each piece of bread and bake in a preheated 400° oven for 2 to 3 minutes until topping is warm.

# TOMATO BASIL CROSTINI

*Fresh basil is best in this variation of a traditional crostini.*

4 slices *Garlic Basil Bread*, page 28, or *Tomato Basil Bread*, page 30
olive oil for brushing
4 Italian (Roma) tomatoes
1 tsp. (2 cloves) minced garlic
4-6 fresh basil leaves, or 1-1½ tsp. dried
¼ cup freshly grated Parmesan cheese

Follow directions for making crostini on page 32. Briefly chop tomatoes with a food processor. Add garlic, basil and Parmesan and process until well blended. Spread a spoonful of topping on each crostini.

**VARIATION**
Replace Parmesan cheese with ½ cup crumbled feta cheese.

# GINGER SHRIMP CROSTINI

Yield: 16

*The combination of shrimp with ginger and coconut is a real winner on the crostini or as a dip in the **Onion Bread Bowl**, page 47. Makes about 1 cup of dip.*

4 slices *Coconut Bread*, page 20, or leftover plain or herbed bread
olive oil for brushing
½ lb. cooked shrimp, peeled and deveined
½ tsp. (1 clove) minced garlic
2 tsp. grated ginger root
1 scallion, finely chopped
½ tsp. crushed red pepper flakes
2 tbs. orange juice
¼ cup shredded coconut

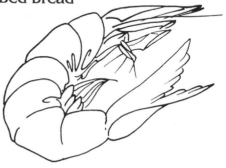

Follow directions for making crostini on page 32. Briefly chop shrimp with a food processor. Add remaining ingredients and process until well blended. Spread each crostini with a spoonful topping.

# CRAB CROSTINI

*These are perfect appetizers when crabs are plentiful.*

4 slices *Rye Bread,* page 25, *Onion Bread,* page 26, *Caraway Bread,* page 24, or
    any leftover plain or herbed bread
olive oil for brushing
1 scallion, chopped (white and green part)
2 oz. (1/2 cup) grated sharp cheddar cheese
4-6 drops Tabasco Sauce
4 oz. crabmeat
chopped almonds

Follow directions for making crostini on page 32.
Process scallion, cheese, Tabasco and crabmeat with a
food processor until finely chopped and blended. Spread
a spoonful on each piece of bread and top with a few almonds.

# MEXICAN CROSTINI

Yield: 16

*Fresh cilantro is really necessary for flavor with this variation. It is found in most grocery stores in the produce section next to the parsley.*

4 slices *Spicy Cheese Cornmeal Bread*, page 27, or any leftover plain bread
olive oil for brushing
1-2 Roma (Italian) tomatoes, thinly sliced
2-3 tbs. minced red onion
¼ cup chopped cilantro
½ tsp. coarsely ground black pepper

Follow directions for making crostini on page 32. Briefly chop tomatoes with a food processor. Add remaining ingredients and process until well blended. Spread each crostini with a spoonful of topping.

# PEPPERONI POCKETS

*These are an absolute crowd pleaser! Buy the pepperoni in large sticks if you can find it.*

**DOUGH**

1 cup water
3 tbs. butter or margarine
1/4 cup sugar

1 tsp. salt
3 cups bread flour
1 1/2 tsp. yeast

**FILLING**

1 lb. pepperoni stick

Make the dough on the dough/manual cycle of the bread machine. Cut pepperoni into 16 slices. Upon completion of the dough cycle, form dough into 16 equal balls. Press each ball between the palms of your hands to flatten. Press a piece of pepperoni into the center and pull sides of dough around it to encase it, pinching with your fingers to seal lightly. Place on a greased baking sheet, cover and let rise for about 30 minutes. Bake in a preheated 350° oven for 15 to 18 minutes or until golden brown.

# PROSCUITTO AND CHEESE KNOTS

Yield: 12

*Any cooked ham can be substituted, although proscuitto does provide a distinctly Italian flavor. These make a wonderful presentation on a buffet table of appetizers, or serve them as fancy dinner rolls. Try garlic-flavored olive oil for brushing.*

## DOUGH

²⁄₃ cup water
2 tbs. olive oil
2 oz. (½ cup) grated
    mozzarella cheese

1 tbs. sugar
½ tsp. salt

2 cups all-purpose flour
1½ tsp. yeast

## FILLING

6 oz. proscuitto or ham, minced
olive oil for brushing

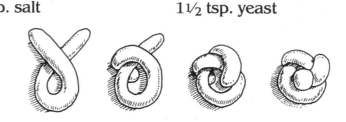

Make dough on the dough/manual cycle of the bread machine. Upon completion of the dough cycle, divide dough into 12 equal pieces. Roll each piece into a small rectangle, about 8 to 10 inches long. Sprinkle with proscuitto and roll jelly roll-style. Tie a loose knot with long ends. Bring one end over and under the roll and the other end up and over, and then tuck each end into the center of the knot. Place knots on a greased baking sheet, cover and let rise for about 30 to 40 minutes. Brush top with olive oil and bake in a preheated 350° oven for 12 to 15 minutes or until golden brown.

# FOCACCIA

*Focaccia (foh-CAH-chee-ah) breads owe their roots to early Italian bakers who used leftover bread dough to make small treats for children. The dough was flattened into a small circle. Fresh herbs (usually either basil or rosemary) were pressed into the top, olive oil was liberally drizzled all over and it was sprinkled with coarse salt. Focaccia can be served hot or cold as an appetizer or side bread with any meal; thick focaccias can be split in half and filled for sandwiches. Use these directions to make the focaccia recipes on the following pages.*

Make dough on the dough/manual cycle of the bread machine. Preheat oven to 350° or 400°, depending on the recipe. Grease a pizza or cookie pan with olive oil or nonstick vegetable spray. A perforated pizza pan gives the bottom crust more crunch.

Upon completion of the dough cycle, remove dough and either roll or stretch and pat it into a 12-inch square or circle. Place dough on greased pan, cover with a kitchen towel and place in a warm, draft-free location to rise for about 30 minutes.

Prepare topping and set aside. After dough has risen, using your fingertips, press small pieces of garlic, onions, nuts, herbs, etc., into dough, making indentations. Drizzle with olive oil (or spray with water for diet or health reasons) and sprinkle with coarse salt. Bake according to the directions in each recipe.

Cut into pie-shaped wedges or bite-sized pieces to serve warm or at room temperature.

# TRADITIONAL GARLIC AND HERB FOCACCIA Makes: 16 slices

*A traditional focaccia uses fresh basil or rosemary; use any favorite herb such as mint, cilantro, rosemary or even parsley.*

## BASIC FOCACCIA DOUGH

1⅛ cups water
1 tbs. olive oil
1 tbs. sugar

½ tsp. salt
3 cups bread flour
1½ tsp. active dry yeast

## TRADITIONAL TOPPING

2-3 cloves garlic, finely slivered or
    minced, or ¼ cup finely slivered
    red onion
2-4 tbs. freshly chopped herbs

¼ cup pine nuts or chopped walnuts,
    optional
1-2 tbs. olive oil
coarse salt to taste

Follow directions for making focaccia on page 39. Press garlic or onion slivers, chopped fresh herbs and nuts, if using, deeply into dough with your fingers. Drizzle with olive oil and sprinkle with coarse salt. Bake focaccia on the bottom rack in a preheated 400° oven for 20 minutes. Cut into 16 slices.

# CILANTRO FOCACCIA

*Cilantro is used in cooking literally all over the world. In the Americas, it is most often used in Mexican cooking. It is now available in just about every grocery store produce section in the US.*

## CILANTRO FOCACCIA DOUGH

1 cup water
1 tbs. olive oil
1 tsp. (2 cloves) minced garlic
1 tsp. minced ginger root, optional
1/4 cup chopped cilantro

1 tbs. sugar
1/2 tsp. salt
3 cups bread flour
1 1/2 tsp. yeast

## CILANTRO TOPPING

2-3 cloves garlic, finely slivered or
    minced, or 1/4 cup finely slivered
    red onion

2-4 tbs. chopped cilantro
1-2 tbs. olive oil
coarse salt to taste

Follow directions for making focaccia on page 39. Press garlic or onion slivers and chopped cilantro deeply into dough with your fingers. Drizzle with olive oil and sprinkle with coarse salt. Bake focaccia on the bottom rack in a preheated 400° oven for 20 minutes. Cut into 16 slices.

# CHEESE SCALLION FOCACCIA

Makes: 16 slices

*The combination of a very sharp cheddar cheese with green onion is a favorite of many. The scallions can throw off the consistency of the dough; watch it and add additional water if necessary.*

## SCALLION FOCACCIA DOUGH

1-1⅛ cups water
1 tbs. olive oil
3 scallions, chopped (white and green part)
½ tsp. salt

1 tbs. sugar
3 cups bread flour
1½ tsp. yeast

## CHEESE TOPPING

1 oz. (¼ cup) grated sharp cheddar cheese
1 tbs. olive oil
coarse salt to taste

Follow directions for making focaccia on page 39. Press pieces of cheese deeply into dough. Drizzle with olive oil and sprinkle with coarse salt. Bake focaccia on the middle rack of a preheated 350° oven for 20 minutes. Cut into 16 slices.

# SPICY MEXICAN FOCACCIA

*This is a very spicy and flavorful focaccia which easily stands alone as an appetizer or accompanies a light soup and salad meal.*

## MEXICAN FOCACCIA DOUGH

1¼ cups water
1 tbs. olive oil
¾ tsp. salt
1½ tsp. crushed red pepper flakes, or
    ½ tsp. cayenne pepper

½-1 tsp. coarsely ground black pepper
1 tbs. sugar
⅓ cup cornmeal
3 cups bread flour
1½ tsp. yeast

## SPICY TOPPING

2-3 cloves garlic, finely slivered, or
    ¼ cup finely slivered red onion
sliced or diced jalapeño peppers to taste
1-2 tbs. chopped cilantro

1-2 tbs. grated sharp cheddar cheese,
    optional
1-2 tbs. olive oil
coarse salt to taste

Follow directions for making focaccia on page 39. Press garlic or onion slivers, jalapeños, cilantro and cheese, if using, deeply into dough with your fingers. Drizzle with olive oil and sprinkle with coarse salt. Bake focaccia on the bottom rack in a preheated 400° oven for 20 minutes. Cut into 16 slices.

# DIPS IN BREAD BOWLS

*These are incredibly easy to make and guaranteed to receive rave reviews. The bread can be made a day ahead. A 9-inch baking dish makes a lower, wider bread bowl for dipping, and a soufflé dish makes a more compact, higher rising and deeper bread bowl. Use the bread cubes as dippers.*

Make the dough on the dough/manual cycle of the bread machine. Upon completion of the cycle, place dough on a lightly floured surface. Shape into a large ball and place in a well-greased 9-inch round baking dish or a 7½- to 8-inch round, deep soufflé dish. Cover with a towel and place in a warm, draft-free location to rise until doubled in bulk, about 1 to 1½ hours for rye bread and 45 to 60 minutes for herb bread. Brush the top with a little olive oil and bake in a preheated 350° oven for about 30 to 40 minutes, or until golden brown and bread sounds hollow when tapped. Remove and cool on a wire rack.

When completely cool, remove the top of the bread with a serrated knife and remove the center, leaving a shell about ½-inch thick on sides and bottom. Make 1 to 1½-inch-deep cuts around the rim every 1½ to 2 inches. Brush the inside surface with a little olive oil. Cut removed bread into 1-inch cubes and brush with olive oil. Place bread bowl and bread cubes on a greased baking sheet and dry in a 200° oven for about 2 hours. If making in advance, the bread can be kept in a tin or paper bag.

# BRIE IN AN HERBED BREAD BOWL

Dip yield: 2 cups

*Use your favorite herb in the bread: parsley, mint, cilantro, basil, oregano, etc.*

**GARLIC HERB DOUGH**

1 cup water
2 tbs. olive oil
1 tsp. (2 cloves) minced garlic
1/4 cup finely chopped fresh herbs, or
    1 tbs. dried

1/2 tsp. salt
2 tbs. sugar
3 cups bread flour
2 tsp. yeast

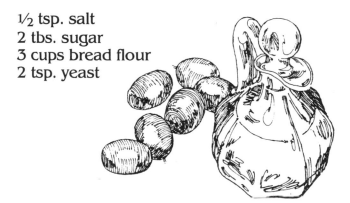

**BRIE DIP**

olive oil
1 lb. Brie cheese
fresh herbs for garnish, optional

Follow directions on page 44 to make the bread bowl. Remove rind from Brie and cut into 1-inch cubes. Fill bread shell with cheese cubes; set aside until ready to bake. Bake in a preheated 350° oven for 15 to 20 minutes or until cheese melts. Serve immediately with bread cubes for dipping, garnished with a few sprigs of fresh herbs, if desired.

# SPINACH DIP IN A RYE BREAD BOWL

Dip yield: 2 cups

*This bread dough rises for quite a long time due to the large amount of rye flour.*

## RYE DOUGH

1 1/3 cups water
3 tbs. olive oil
1/2 tsp. salt
2 tbs. sugar
1 tbs. dill seed

1 tbs. unsweetened cocoa powder
1 1/2 cups rye flour
2 cups bread flour
2 tsp. yeast

## SPINACH DIP

1 pkg. (10 oz.) frozen chopped spinach
1 cup cottage cheese (can be nonfat)
1/4 cup mayonnaise (can be light)
2-3 scallions, chopped (white and green part)

1 oz. (1/4 cup) crumbled feta cheese, optional
1/2 tsp. (1 clove) minced garlic
1/2 tsp. salt
1 tsp. black pepper

Follow directions on page 44 to make the bread bowl. Thaw spinach and drain in a colander. Mix together all remaining dip ingredients with a food processor or electric mixer. Squeeze spinach very dry and mix into dip ingredients, processing briefly until blended. Refrigerate for 1 to 24 hours. Just before serving, spoon dip into bread bowl. Serve with bread cubes for dipping.

# CRAB DIP IN AN ONION BREAD BOWL

Dip yield: 2-2½ cups

*This dip is also terrific in a **Rye Bread Bowl**, page 46. Use reduced fat and nonfat products in the dip to lower calories. Regular dry mustard can be substituted.*

## ONION DOUGH

1 cup water
2 tbs. olive oil
¼ cup chopped onion
1 tbs. sugar

1 tsp. salt
3 cups bread flour
2 tsp. yeast

## CRAB DIP

8 oz. cream cheese, softened
½ cup sour cream
¼ cup mayonnaise
1 tbs. horseradish
½ tsp. dry Oriental mustard

½ tsp. Worcestershire sauce
few drops Tabasco Sauce
8 oz. crabmeat
4 oz. (1 cup) grated cheddar cheese

Follow directions on page 44 to make the bread bowl. Process cheese, sour cream, mayonnaise, horseradish, mustard, Worcestershire and Tabasco with an electric mixer or food processor until well blended. Add crabmeat and cheese and process briefly until just blended. Refrigerate tightly covered until ready to use. Just before serving, spoon dip mixture into bread bowl. Serve with bread cubes for dipping.

# MINI PIZZAS

*Pizza is an absolute favorite, and the combinations of doughs and toppings are endless (for more, see my book, **THE BEST PIZZA is made at home**). This basic, no frills dough recipe is for a thin crust and may be used with different sauces or cheeses for delightful appetizers. For best results, don't overload the pizzas with sauce or cheese, or they become messy to eat.*

## PIZZA DOUGH
1 cup water
2 tbs. olive oil
1/2 tsp. salt
3 cups bread flour
1 1/2 tsp. yeast

Make dough using the dough/manual cycle of your machine. Upon completion of the cycle, remove dough and roll it into a large rectangle on a lightly floured surface. With a 3-inch biscuit cutter, cut out mini crusts and place on a greased, perforated pizza pan. Spread about 1 tsp. sauce evenly on each, leaving a 1/4-inch border. Top with about 1 tbs. cheese. Loosely cover with plastic wrap and refrigerate up to 8 hours. Dough will rise slightly. Bake in a preheated 500° oven for about 5 minutes.

## TOPPINGS
pizza sauce with grated mozzarella, provolone and Parmesan cheeses
salsa with grated mozzarella and cheddar cheeses
pesto with or without grated mozzarella cheese
pesto with tomato slice
herbed cheese spread
brush with olive oil and top with tomato slice, chopped basil and garlic

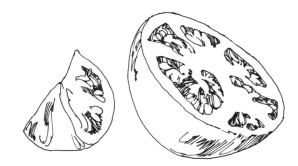

# CHEESE FONDUES

*Bread and cheese-based fondues make an enjoyable appetizer. Choose cheddar or Swiss fondue to accompany a variety of flavored breads. Cut the slices extra-thick and include a piece of crust with each bite. Fondue pots range in price from fairly inexpensive on up. They often come with long-handled forks for spearing bread to dip into the cheese sauce. A chafing dish can be used in lieu of a fondue pot.*

1 loaf *Rye Bread*, page 25, *Onion Bread*, page 26, *Garlic Basil Bread*, page 28, *Garlic Parsley Bread*, page 29, or *Spicy Cheese Cornmeal Bread*, page 27, cut into bite-sized pieces

## CHEDDAR FONDUE

1 tbs. olive or canola oil
1 tsp. (2 cloves) minced garlic
1 cup whole milk, light cream or
    half-and-half

1/4-1/2 tsp. crushed red pepper flakes
4 oz. (1 cup) grated mozzarella cheese
4 oz. (1 cup) grated cheddar cheese

In the top of a double boiler over boiling water, heat oil and cook garlic until tender, about 1 minute. Stir in milk and cook over medium heat for 3 to 5 minutes. Remove from heat and stir in red pepper flakes and cheeses until cheese melts. Pour into a fondue pot and serve over heat with bread cubes.

## SWISS FONDUE
1 tsp. cornstarch
2 tbs. kirsch, light rum, dry sherry or dry white wine
1 clove garlic, cut in half
2 cups dry white wine
1 lb. Swiss cheese, or 8 oz. each Emmentaler cheese and Gruyère cheese, grated
nutmeg or mace

In a small cup or bowl, whisk cornstarch into kirsch until well blended and set aside. Rub inside of fondue pot or a medium saucepan with garlic. Add wine and heat over medium-high heat. Slowly add cheese, stirring constantly. As soon as cheese begins to thicken, add kirsch, mixing well, and cook for about 2 to 3 more minutes. Set fondue pot over heat, or transfer mixture to a chafing dish. Sprinkle with nutmeg or mace.

# BREAKFAST ENTRÉES
# FROM YOUR BREAD MACHINE

# ABOUT BREAKFAST ENTRÉES

Whether you have weekend guests or you want to put a special breakfast on the table for your family, these easy breakfast recipes are ready first thing in the morning with no fuss or hassle.

Make the doughs for coffeecakes and rolls in the machine the evening before. Fill and shape the rolls upon completion of the dough cycle and put them in the refrigerator to rise overnight. In the morning, take the dough out of the refrigerator and preheat the oven. In less than 30 minutes, you can enjoy fresh hot rolls or buns.

If you would rather make the rolls or buns in the morning, follow the recipe directions up to the point at which the dough is put in the refrigerator. Cover the dough with a towel and place it in a warm, draft-free location to rise until doubled, usually 30 to 45 minutes for rolls. Bake as directed in the recipe.

The French toast variations are also easy last-minute throw-togethers. They are a great use for leftover breads or slices that have been frozen. The soaking mixtures can be increased or decreased to fit your needs. The Spanish toasts which tend to be fried in oil are best suited for weekends or days when you are not rushing out the door.

Cooked pieces of French-style toasts can be individually wrapped and frozen. Thaw first and heat them in a 350° oven until warm and crisp.

For decorative toast that's fun to serve, cook the soaked bread in a warm waffle iron or sandwich maker instead of on a griddle.

# CINNAMON BREAKFAST BUNS

Yield: 16

*Cinnamon buns are a classic all-time favorite. While there are plenty of recipes available, I would be remiss not to include one in this book. The dough for this variation is made the evening before and rises overnight, so it can be enjoyed fresh and hot any morning of the week, with no fuss.*

## DOUGH
1⅛ cups milk
2 tbs. butter or margarine
1 tsp. vanilla or almond extract
½ tsp. salt
¼ cup sugar
3 cups all-purpose flour
1½ tsp. yeast

## CINNAMON FILLING
2 tbs. butter or margarine
¼ cup sugar
1 tbs. cinnamon

Make dough on the dough/manual cycle of the bread machine. About 5 minutes before the end of the dough cycle, melt butter or margarine. Upon completion of the dough cycle, roll dough into a 10-x-15-inch rectangle on a lightly floured surface. Brush butter over dough, leaving a ½-inch border all the way around. Mix together sugar and cinnamon and sprinkle evenly over butter-covered dough.

Roll dough jelly roll-style and cut into 16 slices. Place pieces about 1 inch apart on a buttered baking sheet, cover loosely with plastic wrap and refrigerate to rise overnight. In the morning, remove pan from refrigerator and preheat oven to 350°. Bake for 15 to 18 minutes. If desired, drizzle *Glaze* over buns while still warm.

## GLAZE (OPTIONAL)
¼ cup confectioners' sugar
1 tsp. vanilla extract
1-2 tbs. milk or cream

Mix ingredients, adding milk or cream slowly until desired consistency is obtained. (Or make *Glaze* the night before and store in a covered container in the refrigerator. Remove it when you take out the dough in the morning and let it sit at room temperature until you use it.)

# ALMOND POPPY SEED BUNS

Yield: 16

*Select either of the two fillings to complement the poppy seed dough.*

## DOUGH

1⅛ cups milk
2 tbs. butter or margarine
1 tsp. almond extract
1 tbs. poppy seeds

¼ cup sugar
1 tsp. salt
3 cups all-purpose flour
1½ tsp. yeast

Make dough on the dough/manual cycle of the bread machine. At the same time, prepare filling of choice. Upon completion of the dough cycle, roll dough into a 10-x-15-inch rectangle on a lightly floured surface. Spread filling over dough, leaving a ½-inch border all the way around. Roll dough jelly roll-style and cut into 16 slices. Place slices about 1 inch apart on a buttered baking sheet, cover loosely with plastic wrap and place in the refrigerator to rise overnight. In the morning, remove pan from refrigerator and preheat oven to 350°. Bake for 15 to 18 minutes for *Basic Almond Filling*, or 20 to 25 minutes for *Creamy Almond Filling*.

## BASIC ALMOND FILLING
2 tbs. butter, melted
1/4 cup brown sugar, firmly packed
1 tsp. almond extract
1/2 cup finely chopped almonds

Combine melted butter and sugar; add extract. Spread over dough and sprinkle with almonds.

## CREAMY ALMOND FILLING
1/4 cup butter
1/2 cup confectioners' sugar
1 tsp. dried or grated fresh lemon peel (zest), or to taste
1 tsp. almond extract
1 cup sliced almonds

Cream butter and sugar together. Add remaining ingredients, mixing well.

# WALNUT BUNS

Yield: 16

*Both fillings are jam-packed with walnuts, and both are sticky — finger-licking good!*

## DOUGH

¾ cup milk
2 tbs. butter or walnut oil
2 tbs. sugar
½ tsp. salt
2 cups all-purpose flour
1 tsp. yeast

Make dough on the dough/manual cycle of the bread machine. At the end of the dough cycle, remove dough to a lightly floured surface and roll into a 10-x-15-inch rectangle. Spread filling evenly over dough, leaving a ½-inch border all the way around. Roll dough jelly roll-style and cut into 16 slices. Place slices about 1 inch apart on a buttered baking sheet, cover loosely with plastic wrap and place in the refrigerator to rise overnight. In the morning, remove pan from refrigerator and preheat oven to 350°. Bake for 15 to 18 minutes.

## HONEY WALNUT FILLING
1/4 cup sugar
1/4 cup honey
1 cup finely chopped walnuts

Mix together sugar and honey. Add walnuts and stir until well blended.

## GOOEY WALNUT FILLING
1/4 cup butter or margarine, softened
1 cup brown sugar, packed
1 tsp. cinnamon
1 egg
2 cups finely chopped walnuts

Cream butter, sugar and cinnamon together with an electric mixer. Add egg and walnuts and mix until well blended.

# GREEK CHEESE CRESCENTS

Yield: 8

*These cheese crescents are traditionally only eaten on Easter morning; however, we enjoy them any day of the year. The grated cheese should be lightly packed into the measuring cup.*

**DOUGH**

¾ cup milk
2 tbs. olive or vegetable oil
2 tsp. sugar
1 tsp. salt
2 cups all-purpose flour
1½ tsp. yeast

**FILLING**

4 oz. (1 cup) grated cheddar cheese
4 oz. (1 cup) grated mozzarella cheese
4 fresh mint leaves, chopped, or to taste
1 egg

**WASH**

1 egg, beaten with 1-2 tbs. milk or cream

**TOPPING**
sesame seeds

   Make dough on the dough/manual cycle of the bread machine. At the same time, mix filling ingredients together and set aside.

   Remove dough from machine upon completion of the dough cycle. Use a rolling pin to flatten dough into a large circle on a lightly floured surface. With a knife or pizza or pastry wheel, cut dough as you would a pie into 8 triangular pieces. Spread $\frac{1}{8}$ of the filling in the center of the outer edge of each triangle. Roll dough from the outer edge to the point, pressing and sealing filling into dough as you roll. Curve to shape into crescents and place each point side down on a buttered baking sheet. Cover loosely with plastic wrap and refrigerate overnight. In the morning, remove pan from refrigerator and preheat oven to 350°. Brush each crescent with egg wash, sprinkle with sesame seeds and bake for about 12 to 15 minutes, or until golden brown.

# SESAME CHEESE CRESCENTS

Yield: 8

*Not only do these crescents make wonderful breakfast treats with coffee, but they can also be used as dinner rolls with roast lamb or beef.*

## DOUGH
2/3 cup water
2 tbs. olive oil
1 tbs. anise seeds
2 tbs. sesame seeds

2 tbs. sugar
1/2 tsp. salt
2 cups all-purpose flour
1 1/2 tsp. yeast

## FILLING
4 oz. (1 cup) crumbled feta cheese
4 oz. (1 cup) grated mozzarella cheese
1 egg

## WASH
1 egg, beaten with 1-2 tbs. milk or cream

## TOPPING
sesame seeds

Make dough on the dough/manual cycle of the bread machine. At the same time, mix together filling ingredients until well blended and set aside.

Remove dough from machine upon completion of the dough cycle. Use a rolling pin to flatten dough into a large circle on a lightly floured surface. With a knife or pizza or pastry wheel, cut dough as you would a pie into 8 triangular pieces. Spread ⅛ of the filling in the center of the outer edge of each triangle. Roll dough from outer edge to the point, pressing and sealing filling into dough as you roll. Curve to shape into crescents and place each point side down on a buttered baking sheet. Cover loosely with plastic wrap and refrigerate overnight. In the morning, remove pan from refrigerator and preheat oven to 350°. Brush each crescent with egg wash and sprinkle with sesame seeds. Bake for about 15 minutes or until golden brown.

# APPLE PULL-APART
Yield: 16

*This is perfect for a fall or holiday breakfast or brunch. Any dried fruit can be substituted. If your dough cycle does not have a beep to add raisins, add the dried apple to the dough after the dough has kneaded for about 5 minutes (see page 5).*

## DOUGH
⅔ cup apple juice
1 tbs. vegetable oil
2 tbs. maple syrup
½ tsp. salt

2 cups all-purpose flour
1 tsp. yeast
*½ cup chopped dried apple

## TOPPING
½ cup finely chopped walnuts
2 tbs. brown sugar, firmly packed

3 tbs. butter
2 tbs. maple syrup

Make dough on the dough/manual cycle of the bread machine. Remove dough from machine upon completion of the dough cycle and form into 16 equal balls. Place in 4 rows of 4 in a buttered 9-inch square baking dish, cover with plastic wrap and refrigerate overnight. In the morning, remove pan from refrigerator and preheat oven to 350°. Sprinkle dough evenly with nuts and brown sugar. Melt butter and stir in maple syrup, mixing well. Drizzle syrup mixture over nuts and dough. Bake for 25 minutes or until golden brown. "Pull apart" into individual portions to serve.

# CINNAMON COFFEECAKE

Servings: 16

*This is an incredibly easy-to-prepare coffeecake. Serve as a breakfast treat or as a dessert (with or without ice cream).*

**DOUGH**

1⅛ cups warm water
2 tbs. butter
½ tsp. salt

3 tbs. sugar
3 cups bread flour
1½ tsp. active dry yeast

**TOPPING**

¼ cup brown sugar, firmly packed
1 tbs. cinnamon

¼ cup chopped walnuts, optional
2-3 tbs. butter or margarine, melted

Make dough on the dough/manual cycle of the bread machine. Upon completion of the dough cycle, remove dough and, with buttered or sprayed hands, press it into a buttered 9-x-13-inch baking pan. Cover with plastic wrap and refrigerate overnight to rise. In the morning, remove dough from refrigerator and preheat oven to 350°. Mix together brown sugar, cinnamon and walnuts, if using. Press mixture deeply into dough with your fingers. Sprinkle with any remaining topping. Drizzle with melted butter. Bake on the middle rack for about 30 minutes.

# ORANGE RAISIN COFFEECAKE

Servings: 16

*This is a delicious alternative to raisin toast for breakfast. For variety, use any dried fruit, or a combination. Dried sweetened cranberries would be wonderful.*

## DOUGH

1⅛ cups orange juice
2 tbs. butter or margarine
½ tsp. salt

1 tsp. dried or grated fresh
   orange peel (zest), or to taste
3 cups bread flour
1½ tsp. yeast

## TOPPING

2 tbs. sugar
1 tsp. dried or grated fresh orange peel
   (zest)

2-3 tbs. raisins
2 tbs. butter or margarine, melted

Make dough on the dough/manual cycle of the bread machine. At the same time, mix together sugar and orange peel, put it in a container, cover tightly and set aside. Upon completion of the dough cycle, with buttered or sprayed hands, press dough into a buttered 9-x-13-inch baking dish. Cover with plastic wrap and refrigerate overnight. In the morning, remove dough from refrigerator and preheat oven to 350°. Press raisins deeply into dough. Sprinkle with orange sugar and drizzle evenly with melted butter. Bake on the middle rack for about 30 minutes.

# ALMOND APRICOT COFFEECAKE

Servings: 16

*This delicious combination of almonds and apricots is a sure winner for breakfast.*

## DOUGH

1⅛ cups orange juice
2 tbs. butter or margarine
1 tsp. almond extract
1 tbs. sugar

½ tsp. salt
3 cups bread flour
1½ tsp. yeast

## TOPPING

¼ cup finely chopped apricots
2-3 tbs. sliced almonds

1-2 tbs. almond paste
2 tbs. butter or margarine, melted

Make dough on the dough/manual cycle of the bread machine. Upon completion of the dough cycle, with buttered or sprayed hands, press dough into a buttered 9-x-13-inch baking dish. Cover with plastic wrap and refrigerate overnight. In the morning, remove dough from refrigerator and preheat oven to 350°. Press apricots and almonds deeply into dough. Break off small pieces of almond paste and press firmly into dough. Drizzle with melted butter. Bake on the middle rack for about 30 minutes.

# SUGAR GALETTE

*French galettes can be plain or filled with anything from sugar to fruits to meats. The high egg and butter content, which provides much of the liquid for this dough, will result in a low rising dough. It may be necessary to add a tablespoon or two more flour to get dough to form a ball, but be careful to not add too much — the dough should be soft and slightly sticky. Add flavoring to the sugar in the topping (to taste) for variety.*

## DOUGH

½ cup milk
1 egg
2 tbs. butter
¼ cup sugar
½ tsp. salt

1 tsp. dried or grated fresh lemon or orange peel (zest), optional
2 cups all-purpose flour
2 tsp. yeast

## TOPPING

2 tbs. sugar
2 tbs. butter, chilled

1 tsp. grated fresh lemon or orange peel (zest), or to taste, or 1 tsp. cinnamon to taste, optional

Make dough on the dough/manual cycle of the bread machine. At the same time, cut butter into 6 equal slices and return to refrigerator until needed. Upon completion of dough cycle, divide dough into 6 equal pieces. Roll each piece into a 6-inch round and place 1 slice of butter in the center of each round. Sprinkle 1 tsp. sugar evenly over dough, leaving a 2-inch border unsprinkled. Fold one section of border over to cover the outer edge of sprinkled surface and pinch dough to form a rim. Repeat around edge of each galette. The center will not have a dough covering. Place galettes on a buttered baking pan. Cover loosely with plastic wrap and refrigerate overnight to rise. In the morning, remove dough from refrigerator and allow to come to room temperature. Preheat oven to 350°. Bake for about 20 minutes or until crust is golden brown.

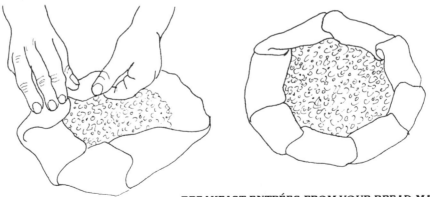

# STRAWBERRY BREAKFAST PUDDING

Servings: 4

*This recipe is based on a dessert pudding which soaks for 8 hours (or overnight) in the refrigerator. I put it together in the evening and enjoy it as a well-rounded (grain, fruit and dairy) breakfast treat in the morning. This can also be prepared in the morning for evening dessert (with or without the banana) and served with yogurt, ice cream or whipped cream.*

1 pkg. (10 oz.) frozen strawberries in sweetened syrup, thawed, or 1 qt. fresh
    strawberries, sliced, with ½ cup sugar
3-4 slices *Orange Bread*, page 17, *Coconut Bread*, page 20, or *French Walnut
    Bread*, page 23, or any leftover sweet bread
1 banana
plain or flavored yogurt

If strawberries are frozen, thaw well. If strawberries are fresh, mix briefly with sugar in a medium bowl and let sit for several hours until a syrup is made. Remove crusts from bread. Cut or break bread into 1-inch cubes and distribute evenly into 4 dessert bowls or glasses. Divide strawberries and syrup evenly among dishes and mix each one well. Cover tightly with plastic wrap and refrigerate overnight or for at least 8 hours. Top with sliced banana and yogurt to serve.

# SPANISH FRIED BREAD

Servings: 4

*This is based on a Spanish recipe which is traditionally served with a syrup made from lemon peel. I put the lemon flavoring in the bread and serve it with lemon curd or fruit-flavored syrups, such as apricot.*

1/2 cup milk
1/4-1/3 cup honey
2 eggs, beaten
4 slices *Lemon Bread*, page 16, or any leftover plain or sweet bread
vegetable oil for frying, optional
lemon curd or fruit syrup, such as apricot

Mix together milk, honey and beaten eggs. Place bread side by side in a large, shallow pan and pour milk mixture on top. Turn slices of bread several times to coat well and let sit for 5 to 10 minutes. Fry on each side in hot oil (about 1/2-inch in a skillet, or a full deep fryer) until golden brown. Serve warm with lemon curd or fruit syrup.

**LOW FAT TIP:** Use nonfat milk and egg substitute. Instead of frying, cook on a nonstick griddle as you would French toast.

# SPANISH TOAST BITES

Servings: 4

*Similar to **Spanish Fried Bread**, page 71, the Spanish also eat small fried bites of bread served with confectioners' sugar or a cinnamon sugar mixture (my kids' favorite).*

4 slices *Orange Bread*, page 17, or any leftover plain or sweet bread
1-1½ cups milk
¼ tsp. salt
olive or vegetable oil for frying
½ cup all-purpose or bread flour
confectioners' sugar or cinnamon sugar (¼ cup sugar mixed with 1 tbs. cinnamon)

Break or cut bread into bite-sized chunks and place in a bowl. Mix milk with salt and pour over bread — there should be enough milk to soak bread, but not enough to make bread float. While bread is soaking, heat oil in a deep fryer or about 1 inch of oil in a large skillet. Remove bread cubes from milk and place on a plate or in a shallow pan. Sprinkle with flour to coat cubes. Fry in deep fryer or skillet over medium heat until golden. Drain on paper towels and serve warm with confectioners' sugar or cinnamon sugar.

# SPANISH TOAST

*This French-style toast is based on a Spanish recipe. Cut 4 fairly thick slices of your leftover bread. The soaking mixture can easily be doubled or tripled for more toast.*

2 eggs, beaten
1/2 cup milk
2 tbs. sugar
1/2 tsp. dried or grated fresh lemon or orange peel (zest), or to taste
nutmeg, mace or cinnamon to taste
4 slices *Lemon Bread*, page 16, or *Orange Bread*, page 17, or any leftover sweet
    bread
melted butter, optional
confectioners' sugar
toasted slivered almonds

Mix together eggs, milk, sugar, peel and spice of choice. Soak or dip bread in mixture. Cook each slice of bread on both sides on a hot nonstick griddle or in melted butter in a large skillet until golden brown. Serve warm, sprinkled with confectioners' sugar and toasted slivered almonds.

# WALNUT FRENCH TOAST

Servings: 4

*Any stale or leftover bread makes great French toast, but we enjoy using walnuts in the bread for a real French treat.*

2 eggs, beaten
1/4 cup milk
1/2-1 tsp. vanilla extract
cinnamon and/or nutmeg to taste
4 slices *French Walnut Bread*, page 23, *Coconut Bread*, page 20, or any leftover
    plain or sweet bread
walnut oil or melted butter, optional
maple or fruit syrup or confectioners' sugar and toasted walnuts

Mix together eggs, milk, vanilla and cinnamon. Place bread side by side in a large, shallow pan and pour mixture on top. Turn slices of bread several times to coat well and allow to soak for 10 to 15 minutes. Cook each slice of bread on both sides on a hot nonstick griddle or in walnut oil or melted butter in a large skillet until golden brown. Serve warm with maple or fruit syrup, or with confectioners' sugar and toasted walnuts.

# FRENCH TOAST CAJUN-STYLE

Servings: 4

*The Cajuns use a citrus-based soaking mixture instead of milk when they make French toast. This variation complements the citrus flavor with a delicious apricot bread. Watch carefully when cooking to avoid burning.*

4 eggs, beaten
1/2 cup orange juice
1/4 cup sugar
1/2-1 tsp. lemon extract
1 tsp. dried or grated fresh lemon peel (zest), or to taste
4 slices *Apricot Bread*, page 19, or any leftover plain or sweet bread
melted butter, optional
honey, confectioners' sugar or maple syrup

Mix together eggs, orange juice, sugar, extract and peel. Place bread side by side in a large, shallow pan and pour mixture on top. Turn slices of bread several times to coat well and allow to soak for 10 to 15 minutes. Cook each slice of bread on both sides on a hot nonstick griddle or in melted butter in a large skillet until golden brown. Serve warm with honey, confectioners' sugar or syrup.

# HAWAIIAN TOAST

*For a more substantial breakfast, briefly dip slices of ham in the soaking mixture and cook them on the griddle while the bread is soaking. Serve together.*

4 slices *Hawaiian Bread*, page 18, or *Coconut Bread*, page 20, or any leftover plain
    or sweet bread
2 eggs
1 can (6 oz.) pineapple juice
1/4 tsp. ground ginger, or 1 tsp. grated ginger root
butter and brown sugar, or maple syrup

Remove crusts from bread if desired. Place bread in a 9-x-13-inch baking dish. Beat eggs and mix in pineapple juice and ginger. Pour over bread and turn slices of bread several times to coat well. Allow bread to soak for 10 to 15 minutes. Bake on a medium-hot nonstick griddle, cooking each side until brown. Watch carefully to avoid burning.

76  BREAKFAST ENTRÉES FROM YOUR BREAD MACHINE

# BRUNCH AND LUNCH ENTRÉES FROM YOUR BREAD MACHINE

# ITALIAN BREAD SALAD

Servings: 2 as entrée; 4 as side dish

*Based on an Italian recipe for panzanella, this recipe uses a flavorful herb bread instead of a plain ethnic or white bread, which is traditionally used. Use leftover meat to make the salad a hearty lunch meal, or omit it. Either way, the salad is very filling.*

4 slices *Garlic Basil Bread*, page 28, or
    *Tomato Basil Bread*, page 30, or any
    leftover plain or herbed bread
2-3 medium tomatoes, or 6-8 Italian
    (Roma) tomatoes
1/2-1 medium-sized red onion, thinly sliced
chopped fresh basil to taste

1/2 medium cucumber, thinly sliced
1/2 medium bell pepper, thinly sliced
1-1 1/2 cups diced cooked turkey,
    chicken or ham, optional
1/4 cup freshly grated Parmesan cheese
1/4 cup chopped walnuts or pine nuts

## DRESSING
2 tbs. olive oil
3 tbs. red wine vinegar
1/2 tsp. (1 clove) minced garlic, or to taste

salt and coarsely ground black pepper
    to taste

Break or cut bread into bite-sized pieces and place in a large bowl. Chop tomatoes by hand or with a food processor and add to bread, mixing very well. Let sit for 10 to 15 minutes until bread absorbs juice and softens. Add remaining ingredients and mix well. Combine dressing ingredients and toss with salad when ready to serve.

# GREEK BREAD SALAD

Servings: 2 as entrée; 4 as side dish

*Regular Greek salads are among my favorites. This combines the best of both worlds — a bread salad with Greek salad flavors.*

4 slices *Garlic Parsley Bread*, page 29, or any leftover plain or herbed bread
2-3 medium tomatoes, or 6-8 medium Italian (Roma) tomatoes
¼ cup chopped fresh parsley, or to taste
½ bell pepper (any color), finely diced
2 scallions, diced, including green part

1 stalk celery, diced
6 kalamata olives, sliced
1-1½ cups cooked chicken, turkey or lamb, optional
4 oz. (1 cup) crumbled feta cheese
¼ cup sliced almonds

**DRESSING**
2 tbs. olive oil
3 tbs. red wine vinegar
1 tbs. lemon juice
1½ tsp. fresh oregano, or ½ tsp. dried

1 tsp. (2 cloves) minced garlic, or to taste
salt, optional
coarsely ground black pepper to taste

Break or cut bread into bite-sized pieces and place in a large bowl. Chop tomatoes and add to the bread, mixing very well. Let sit for 10 to 15 minutes so the bread soaks up the juice and softens. Add remaining ingredients and mix well. Combine dressing ingredients and toss with salad when ready to serve.

# CARIBBEAN BREAD SALAD

Servings: 2 as entrée; 4 as side dish

*This seems to scream for shrimp, but leftover chicken can be substituted, or the shrimp can simply be omitted.*

4 thick slices *Onion Bread*, page 26
2-3 medium tomatoes, or 6-8 Italian (Roma) tomatoes
1/2-1 medium-sized red onion, very thinly sliced
1/2 medium cucumber, thinly sliced

1/2 medium bell pepper, thinly sliced
1/4 cup chopped cilantro or fresh parsley, or to taste
4-8 oz. cooked, peeled shrimp, diced
1/2 cup freshly grated Parmesan cheese

## DRESSING

2 tbs. olive oil
3 tbs. red wine vinegar
1/2 tsp. ground coriander
1/2 tsp. ground turmeric
1/4 tsp. cumin

1/2 tsp. salt
1/4 tsp. cayenne pepper
1 tsp. grated ginger root, or 1/4 tsp. ground ginger
1 tsp. (2 cloves) minced garlic

Break or cut bread into small, bite-sized pieces and place in a large bowl. Chop tomatoes and add to bread, mixing very well. Let sit for 10 to 15 minutes until bread soaks up juice and softens. Add remaining ingredients and mix well. Combine dressing ingredients and toss with salad when ready to serve.

# MEXICAN BREAD SALAD

Servings: 2 as entrée; 4 as side dish

*With either black beans or chicken, this salad is a winner.*

4 slices *Spicy Cheese Cornmeal Bread*, page 27, or any leftover cheese or spicy bread
2-3 medium tomatoes, or 6-8 Italian (Roma) tomatoes
1/2-1 medium-sized red onion, very thinly sliced (prefer Bermuda)
1 can (15 oz.) black beans, rinsed and drained, or 1-1 1/2 cups diced cooked chicken
2 oz. (1/2 cup) grated Monterey Jack cheese, optional
1/4 cup chopped cilantro, or to taste

## DRESSING
2 tbs. olive oil
3 tbs. tarragon vinegar
1 tsp. lemon juice
1/2 tsp. (1 clove) minced garlic, or to taste

1/2 jalapeño pepper, diced, or to taste
salt and lemon pepper to taste

Break or cut bread into bite-sized pieces and place in a large bowl. Coarsely chop tomatoes and add to bread, mixing very well. Let sit for 10 to 15 minutes so the bread soaks up the juice and softens. Add remaining ingredients and mix well. Toss dressing with salad when ready to serve.

# TURNOVERS

*Whether they are called turnovers, calzones, empanadas, boreks, pockets or any other name, fillings enclosed by dough are enjoyed all over the world. They can be filled with meats, cheeses, fruits or sweets; they can be made with a pastry dough or a yeast-leavened dough. While some ethnic turnovers are traditionally fried, I prefer baking them. They are wonderful for lunch boxes, picnics or casual meals fresh from the oven or cold from the refrigerator. Follow these directions for the turnovers on the following pages.*

1. Make dough on the dough/manual cycle of the bread machine.
2. Prepare the filling as described in the recipe and set aside.
3. Prepare egg wash (if called for): beat an egg white with 1-2 tbs. water.
4. Preheat oven to 375°.
5. Grease a baking sheet with olive oil or spray with nonstick vegetable spray.
6. Upon completion of the dough cycle, divide the dough into the given number of equal pieces.
7. Roll each piece into a 6- to 8-inch diameter circle and brush the outer edge with egg wash or water. Place the filling in the center of the circle and pull one side over the other. Press firmly with your fingers to seal and then crimp edge with the tines of a fork. Pierce the top in 1 or 2 places with the fork to allow steam to escape while baking.

8.  Place the turnovers on a greased baking sheet, brush the tops with egg wash or oil and bake according to the directions in each recipe.
9.  If not baking immediately, cover the turnovers lightly with plastic wrap and refrigerate for up to 4 hours.

Turnovers can also be made in smaller versions for wonderful appetizers. Make the turnovers according to the directions in the recipe, but use the numbers given in parenthesis. For example, if a recipe calls for 12 turnovers, each with $1/4$ cup filling, you can make 24 smaller turnovers, each with 2 tbs. filling — you'll find those measurements in parenthesis in each recipe. If you want to prepare turnovers in advance, place them on the greased baking sheet, cover loosely with plastic wrap and refrigerate for up to 4 hours. Remove the baking sheet from the refrigerator and bake in a preheated oven. The dough will rise slightly in the refrigerator, so you should expect the crust to be slightly thicker than if you baked the turnovers immediately after making.

Turnovers can be reheated in the microwave by wrapping them in a damp paper towel and heating briefly, or they can be wrapped in aluminum foil and heated in a 350° oven for 5 to 10 minutes.

Use any of the doughs and your own imagination for filling ingredients.

# LAMB AND FETA TURNOVERS

Yield: 12 large; 24 small

*Lamb and feta cheese go hand in hand in this Greek-flavored turnover. Greek seasoning blends can be purchased at grocery stores or some Greek restaurants.*

## GARLIC DOUGH

1/8 cups water
1 tbs. olive oil
1 tsp. (2 cloves) minced garlic
1 tsp. sugar

1/2 tsp. salt
3 cups bread flour
1 1/2 tsp. yeast

## LAMB AND FETA FILLING

1 lb. ground lamb
1/4-1/2 cup diced onion
1 tsp. (2 cloves) minced garlic

olive oil for brushing

1 tbs. Greek seasoning, or 2 tsp. dried
    oregano and 1 tsp. basil
8 oz. (2 cups) crumbled feta cheese

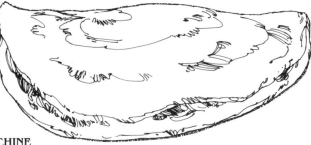

Make dough on the dough/manual cycle of the bread machine. At the same time, cook lamb, onion and garlic in a large skillet until meat is done and onions are soft. Add seasoning and cook for another 1 to 2 minutes. Remove from heat, drain well, mix in feta and set aside.

Follow directions for making 12 (24) turnovers on page 82. Fill each turnover with about ⅓ cup (2½ tbs.) filling. Brush with olive oil. Bake in a preheated 375° oven for about 20 (15) minutes until the top is golden brown. Serve hot, or cool on a wire rack and serve at room temperature.

## VARIATION: HERBED FETA TURNOVERS

For a vegetarian version, omit lamb and chopped onion from the filling and increase amount of feta cheese to 12 oz. Mix in 1 egg. Instead of Greek seasoning in the filling, add ¼ cup chopped fresh herbs to filling and ¼ cup chopped fresh herbs to dough (or 1 heaping tbs. dried); dill, mint, oregano or parsley are favorite choices.

# RICOTTA CALZONES

*I like parsley in these turnovers, but any favorite fresh herb can be substituted.*

## GARLIC PARSLEY DOUGH

1 cup water
2 tbs. olive oil
1 tsp. (2 cloves) minced garlic
½ tsp. salt

2 tbs. chopped fresh parsley
3 cups all-purpose flour
1½ tsp. yeast

## HERBED CHEESE FILLING

1 container (15 oz.) ricotta cheese
1 egg
½ cup freshly grated Parmesan cheese
4 oz. (1 cup) crumbled feta cheese
2 oz. (½ cup) grated mozzarella cheese

2-3 scallions, diced (white and green part)
¼ cup chopped fresh parsley
½ tsp. salt
1 tsp. crushed red pepper flakes or
   black pepper, or to taste

Make dough on the dough/manual cycle of the bread machine. Mix together filling ingredients and set aside. Follow the directions for making 12 (24) turnovers on page 82. Fill each turnover with a scant ¼ cup (2 tbs.) filling. Brush with olive oil or egg wash. Bake in a preheated 375° oven for about 25 (15) minutes until the top is golden brown. Serve hot, or cool on a wire rack and serve at room temperature.

# SAUSAGE CHEESE TURNOVERS

Yield: 12 large; 24 small

*The fennel seeds really perk up the flavor of this favorite combination.*

## FENNEL PEPPER DOUGH

1 cup water
2 tbs. olive oil
1 tsp. (2 cloves) minced garlic
1 tbs. sugar
1 tbs. fennel seeds

$\frac{1}{2}$ tsp. salt
$\frac{1}{2}$ tsp. coarse ground black pepper
3 cups bread flour
1$\frac{1}{2}$ tsp. yeast

## SAUSAGE CHEESE FILLING

12 oz. pork sausage, cooked, drained
   and crumbled

4 oz. (1 cup) grated cheddar cheese
4 oz. (1 cup) grated mozzarella cheese

olive oil for brushing

Make dough on the dough/manual cycle of the bread machine. At the same time, mix together cooked sausage and cheese; set aside.

Follow directions for making 12 (24) turnovers on page 82. Fill each turnover with about $\frac{1}{4}$ cup (2 tbs.) filling. Brush with olive oil. Bake in a preheated 375° oven for about 20 (15) minutes until the top is golden brown. Serve hot, or cool on a wire rack and serve at room temperature.

# HAM AND CHEESE IN MUSTARD RYE POCKETS

Yield: 12 large; 24 small

*Use either the regular dry mustard or seeds found in the spice section of the grocery store. For variety, try a dry, hot Oriental mustard found in the Oriental foods section of the store.*

**MUSTARD RYE DOUGH**

1 cup water
1 tbs. vegetable oil
2 tbs. molasses
1 tsp. ground dry mustard, or 1 tbs.
    mustard seeds

1/2 tsp. salt
1 tbs. unsweetened cocoa powder
1 cup rye flour
2 cups bread flour
2 tsp. yeast

**HAM AND CHEESE FILLING**

1 lb. baked ham
1/2 lb. provolone or Swiss cheese

**WASH**

1 egg, beaten with 1-2 tbs. water

**TOPPING SUGGESTIONS (OPTIONAL)**
mustard seeds
caraway seeds

Make dough on the dough/manual cycle of the bread machine. At the same time, cut ham and cheese into bite-sized pieces. Mix together well and set aside.

Follow the directions for making 8 (16) turnovers on page 82. Fill each turnover with about 1/4 cup (2 tbs.) filling. Brush with egg wash and sprinkle with seeds, if using. Bake in a preheated 375° oven for about 20 to 25 minutes. Serve hot, or cool on a wire rack and serve at room temperature.

# CORNISH PASTIES

*Pasties are a meal-in-one, either hot from the oven or carried in a lunch box or picnic basket. These are a variation of the traditional pasties that Cornish miners once carried in their pockets to work. Feel free to add other vegetables from the garden; peas, bell peppers, etc. Adjust the salt and pepper in the filling to your taste.*

## DOUGH

1 cup water
2 tbs. olive oil
1 tsp. (2 cloves) minced garlic
1/4 cup chopped fresh parsley, or
    1 tbs. dried, crumbled

1/2 tsp. salt
1 tsp. sugar
3 cups bread flour
1 1/2 tsp. yeast

## FILLING

1 lb. ground chuck or turkey
1/4 medium onion
1 medium to large potato, uncooked
1 medium carrot

1/2 tsp. salt
1 tsp. coarse pepper
1 tbs. chopped fresh parsley, or 1 tsp.
    dried

**WASH**
1 egg, beaten with 1-2 tbs. water

Make dough on the dough/manual cycle of the bread machine. At the same time, cook meat and set aside to cool. Process onion, potato and carrot with a food processor until finely chopped. Mix together with cooked meat in a large bowl and add seasonings.

Upon completion of the dough cycle, form dough into 8 equal balls and roll or flatten into rounds. Brush edges of each round with egg wash. Place ½ cup filling in the center of each round. Fold edges of dough together so the seam is on top and pinch closed with your fingers to seal tightly. Place on a greased baking sheet, allowing room for each to expand during cooking without touching. Brush outside of dough with egg wash and pierce each side of the seam with a sharp knife in 2 or 3 places. Bake in a preheated 350° oven for 20 to 25 minutes. Serve hot, or cool on a wire rack and serve at room temperature.

# WELSH RAREBIT FOR KIDS

Servings: 4-6

*This is a basic one for the kids on one of those days (or nights) when you just don't feel like cooking. Keep bread in the freezer (presliced) for real ease. If your child does not like tomatoes, just leave them out. If you have any leftover sauce, it will keep in the refrigerator for a few days and can be rewarmed in the microwave. The processed cheese melts better without clumping, but cheddar has a stronger flavor. Worcestershire, mustard and paprika are all traditional rarebit flavorings. If you have really finicky kids, only add those flavorings to adult portions.*

## RAREBIT SAUCE

2 tbs. butter or margarine
8 oz. (2 cups) grated sharp cheddar
   cheese or processed American cheese
   (such as Velveta)
salt and pepper to taste

1 tsp. Worcestershire sauce, optional
1/2 tsp. dry mustard, optional
1/2 tsp. paprika, optional
1/4-1/3 cup milk

1-2 tomatoes, sliced
4-6 slices *Kids' White Bread*, page 11, toasted

Melt butter in a double boiler over boiling water. Add cheese slowly to butter, stirring constantly. Season with salt, pepper, Worcestershire sauce, mustard and paprika, if using. Slowly stir in milk when cheese has melted. Cook for 1 to 2 minutes. Place a slice of tomato on each piece of toast and cover with warm *Rarebit Sauce*.

**VARIATION: WELSH RAREBIT FOR ADULTS**
Add ½-1 tsp. crushed red pepper flakes to *Rarebit Sauce* and serve over tomato and cooked, hot (spicy) sausage on toast.

# BLACK BEAN CHILI IN BREAD BOWLS

Servings: 6

*These edible bowls can hold a variety of foods, such as thick stews or soups, chili or salads. The herb should complement whatever you plan to serve with it. For example, if you are serving chili or a taco-type salad, use cilantro. If you are serving a thick chicken soup, use oregano or tarragon. If you don't have 10 oz. custard cups, you can use any bowl of similar size and shape; just make sure that the bowl is ovenproof.*

## DOUGH

1 cup water
2 tbs. olive or vegetable oil
½ tsp. (1 clove) minced garlic
1 tbs. chopped fresh herb, or 1 tsp.
    dried, optional

1 tbs. sugar
½ tsp. salt
3 cups bread flour
1½ tsp. yeast

olive or vegetable oil for brushing

Make dough on the dough/manual cycle of the bread machine. Spray or grease a baking sheet and the *outside* of six 10 oz. custard cups and place cups upside down on the baking sheet. Upon completion of the dough cycle, divide dough into 6 equal pieces. Roll each piece on a lightly floured surface into a 6- or 7-inch round and shape each over the outside of the custard cup. If there is excess dough, crimp dough onto baking sheet to form a rim. Brush dough lightly with olive or vegetable oil and bake in a preheated 350° oven for 25 to 28 minutes or until golden brown. Carefully lift bread bowls from cups and completely cool upright on wire racks.

## BLACK BEAN CHILI

1 tbs. olive oil
½ medium onion, chopped
½ green bell pepper, chopped
1 tsp. (2 cloves) minced garlic
1 can (15.5 oz.) black beans, rinsed and drained
1 can (14.5 oz.) chopped tomatoes with juice

1 tsp. chopped jalapeño peppers, or to taste
1 tsp. ground cumin
1 tsp. crushed dried oregano, or 1 tbs. chopped fresh
salt and pepper to taste
1 tbs. red wine vinegar
2-4 drops Tabasco Sauce, or to taste

Heat oil in a large skillet and cook onion, bell pepper and garlic until just tender. Add black beans and remaining ingredients, mixing well. Simmer over medium low heat for 10 to 15 minutes or until heated through. Serve in bread bowls.

# GRILLED CHICKEN SATAY SANDWICHES

Servings: 8

*Satay is an Indonesian specialty of marinated cubes of meat or poultry that are grilled on skewers and served with a spicy peanut sauce. These chicken sandwiches are perfect for a cookout. Everything can be prepared early in the day, leaving you free to enjoy your guests. Or make sandwiches in advance, wrap each one in aluminum foil and take them on a picnic or tailgating. The recipe can easily be doubled or tripled.*

## ROLLS

¾ cup water
1 tbs. sesame oil
¼-½ tsp. ground ginger, or 1-2 tsp.
    grated ginger root

½ tsp. salt
1 tbs. sugar
2 cups all-purpose flour
1½ tsp. yeast

## CHICKEN AND MARINADE

¼ cup soy sauce
2 tbs. sesame oil
2 tbs. lemon juice
1 tsp. (2 cloves) minced garlic
1 tsp. grated ginger root, or ¼ tsp.
    ground ginger

2 drops Tabasco Sauce
salt and pepper to taste
8 boneless chicken breast halves

## SATAY PEANUT SAUCE

⅓ cup creamy peanut butter
¼-⅓ cup unsweetened coconut milk
¼ cup chicken broth
1 tbs. soy sauce
½-1 tsp. diced jalapeño peppers

1 tsp. (2 cloves) minced garlic
1 tsp. grated ginger root, or ¼ tsp.
   ground ginger
¼ tsp. salt, or to taste
½ tsp. pepper, or to taste

Make dough on the dough/manual cycle of the bread machine. Upon completion of the dough cycle, divide dough into 8 equal pieces and shape each piece into a roll. Place on a greased baking sheet, cover and let rise in a warm, draft-free location for about 30 minutes. Bake in a preheated 350° oven for 18 to 20 minutes.

Mix together marinade ingredients and pour over chicken in a plastic or glass container. Cover and refrigerate for 1 to 8 hours.

Process all sauce ingredients with a food processor or blender until smooth. If sauce is made in advance and refrigerated, warm in the microwave for 1 minute and stir until smooth. Serve chicken on a bun with sauce.

# TURKEY STRATA

*The advantage of stratas is that they must be made at least 8 hours ahead. This is an absolutely wonderful lunch or brunch for Thanksgiving weekend guests. You can also make it in the morning and pop it in the oven for dinner with a salad. Craisins (sometimes called crannies) are dried, sweetened cranberries. Raisins can be substituted, but don't seem to add the holiday flair.*

6 eggs
1/4 tsp. salt, or to taste
1/2 tsp. black pepper, or to taste
1 cup milk
4 slices *Cranberry Nut Bread*, page 22,
    or leftover plain or herbed bread

1/4 cup minced onion, optional
1/2 cup craisins or raisins
1/2 cup chopped walnuts, optional
1-1 1/2 cups diced cooked turkey
4 oz. (1 cup) grated cheddar cheese

Beat eggs together, season with salt and pepper and add milk, mixing well; set aside. Break or cut bread into bite-sized pieces and spread evenly in a greased 9-x-13-inch baking pan. Cover, in layers, with onion if using, craisins/raisins, walnuts if using, turkey and cheese. Pour egg and milk mixture on top, cover and refrigerate overnight. Bake covered in a preheated 350° oven for 30 minutes, or until eggs are set.

**NOTE:** To make in a deep, 2-quart casserole, bake about 15 to 20 minutes longer (45 to 50 minutes total).

# HAM AND CHEESE STRATA

*This basic strata made with sweet pineapple bread is good for brunch, or for a light dinner with a salad (spinach with mandarin oranges goes very nicely).*

6 eggs
¼ tsp. salt, or to taste
½ tsp. coarsely ground black pepper, or to taste
½ tsp. ground ginger
1 cup milk

4 slices *Hawaiian Bread*, page 18, or plain or herbed leftover bread
¼ cup minced onion, optional
1-1½ cups diced ham
4 oz. (1 cup) grated cheddar cheese

Beat eggs, season with salt, pepper and ginger and add milk, mixing well; set aside. Break or cut bread into bite-sized pieces and spread on the bottom of a greased 9-x-13-inch baking dish. Cover, in layers, with onion if using, ham and cheese. Pour egg and milk mixture on top, cover and refrigerate overnight. Bake covered in a preheated 350° oven for 30 minutes.

**NOTE:** To make in a deep, 2-quart casserole, bake about 15 to 20 minutes longer (45 to 50 minutes total).

BRUNCH AND LUNCH ENTRÉES FROM YOUR BREAD MACHINE  99

# BROCCOLI AND CHEESE STRATA

Servings: 6

*This is wonderful for brunch or a luncheon, or make it in the morning and serve it with dinner as a side dish.*

1 pkg. (10 oz.) broccoli, chopped or
    florets
6 eggs
¼ tsp. salt, or to taste
¼ tsp. cayenne or black pepper, or to
    taste

1 cup milk
4 slices *Caraway Bread*, page 24, or
    leftover plain or herbed bread
¼ cup minced onion, optional
4 oz. (1 cup) grated cheddar cheese

Cook broccoli according to the directions on the package until broccoli is tender-crisp (do not cook completely); drain and set aside to cool. Beat eggs, season with salt and pepper and add milk, mixing well; set aside. Break or cut bread into bite-sized pieces and spread in a greased 9-x-13-inch baking pan. Cover in layers with onion if using, broccoli and cheese. Pour egg mixture on top, cover and refrigerate overnight. Bake covered in a preheated 350° oven for about 30 minutes.

**NOTE:** To make in a deep, 2-quart casserole, bake about 15 to 20 minutes longer (45 to 50 minutes total).

# CRAB STRATA

*When crabs are plentiful, this can be easily enjoyed as a casual meal (brunch or dinner) with a tossed salad.*

4 eggs
½ tsp. dry mustard
¼ tsp. salt, or to taste
½ tsp. coarsely ground black pepper,
   or to taste
1 cup milk

4 slices *Onion Bread*, page 26, *Garlic
   Parsley Bread*, page 29, or leftover
   plain or herbed bread
8 oz. crabmeat
1-2 stalks celery, chopped
4 oz. (1 cup) grated cheddar cheese

Beat eggs together, season with mustard, salt and pepper and add milk, mixing well; set aside. Break or cut bread into bite-sized pieces and spread on the bottom of a greased 9-x-13-inch baking pan. Cover with crab, celery, and cheese. Pour egg mixture on top, cover and refrigerate overnight. Bake covered in a preheated 350° oven for about 30 minutes.

**NOTE:** To make in a deep, 2-quart casserole, bake about 15 or 20 minutes longer (45 or 50 minutes total).

# CREOLE BREAD PUDDING

Servings: 6-9

*Puddings are more custard-like than stratas, and are made and baked in a water bath just before serving. The sausage can be cooked a day or two in advance.*

4 slices *Onion Bread,* page 26, or
    *Caraway Bread* made with fennel
    seeds instead of caraway, page 24
1/2 lb. hot sausage (Creole or Italian),
    cooked and crumbled
2 cups milk

4 eggs
dash salt
1/2 tsp. dry mustard
1/2-1 tsp. crushed red pepper flakes
3-4 drops Tabasco Sauce
4 oz. (1 cup) grated cheddar cheese

Break bread into bite-sized pieces and spread evenly in a greased 8-inch square baking pan. Spread sausage evenly on top. Bring milk to a boil, remove from heat and set aside. Beat eggs and slowly add to milk, stirring constantly; stir in salt, mustard, red pepper flakes and Tabasco. Pour egg-milk mixture over bread and sausage. Sprinkle with cheese. Place the baking pan in a larger pan and fill larger pan with hot water about halfway up sides of smaller pan. Bake in a preheated 350° oven for about 45 to 50 minutes, or until a knife inserted in the center comes out clean. Serve warm.

# MEXICAN BREAD PUDDING

Servings: 6

*The amount of diced jalapeño peppers can be adjusted, depending on how much "heat" you want. If you remove the seeds, the pepper will be milder.*

4 slices *Spicy Cheese Cornmeal Bread*, page 27
½ lb. cooked ground beef or turkey with taco seasoning
2 cups milk
4 eggs
¼ tsp. salt, or to taste

½ tsp. coarsely ground black pepper, or to taste
½ tsp. diced jalapeño peppers, or to taste
¼ cup minced onion
4 oz. (1 cup) grated cheddar cheese

Break bread into bite-sized pieces and and spread evenly in a greased 8-inch square baking dish. Spread taco-seasoned meat evenly on top. Bring milk to a boil, remove from heat and set aside. Beat eggs and slowly add to milk, stirring constantly; stir in salt, pepper, jalapeños and minced onion. Pour egg-milk mixture over bread and meat and sprinkle with cheese. Place the baking pan in a larger pan and fill larger pan with hot water about halfway up sides of smaller pan. Bake in a preheated 350° oven for about 45 to 50 minutes, or until a knife inserted in the center comes out clean.

# AUSTRIAN EGG CAKE

*This is incredible easy and makes a wonderful presentation. The breadcrumbs can be made a day in advance and kept in a plastic container. Any leftover sweet or herbed bread can be used.*

4 pieces *Lemon Bread*, page 16,
    *Orange Bread*, page 17 or *Hawaiian Bread*, page 18 (about 2 cups fine crumbs)
6 eggs

1½ cups milk
½ tsp. salt
1 tsp. white or black pepper
2-3 scallions, chopped, optional

Remove crusts from bread. Process briefly with a food processor to make fine crumbs. Set aside. With a blender or electric mixer, beat eggs and add milk, salt, pepper, scallions, if using, and breadcrumbs, mixing well. Pour mixture into a greased 2-quart casserole. Place casserole in a larger pan add enough hot water to larger pan to come halfway up sides of casserole. Bake uncovered in a preheated 350° oven for about 45 to 50 minutes, or until eggs are set.

# DUTCH EGG CAKE

*Similar to **Austrian Egg Cake**, page 104, this is richer because of the cream and cheese. Any leftover sweet (fruit-based) bread can be used.*

3 slices *Orange Bread*, page 17
    (1½ cups fine crumbs)
4 eggs
1½ cups light cream or half-and-half
¼ tsp. salt
¼ tsp. white pepper
1 cup (4 oz.) grated Gouda cheese
1 tsp. grated fresh or dried orange
    peel (zest), or to taste

Remove crusts from bread. Process briefly with a food processor to make fine crumbs. Set aside. With a blender or electric mixer, beat eggs and add cream, salt, pepper, breadcrumbs and cheese, mixing well. Pour mixture into a greased 2-quart casserole. Sprinkle with orange peel. Place casserole in a larger pan and add enough hot water to larger pan to come halfway up sides of casserole. Bake uncovered in a preheated 350° oven for 45 to 50 minutes or until eggs are set.

# FOUR-CHEESE QUICHE

Servings: 6

*It's not baked in a traditional round, but this recipe makes a perfect brunch quiche. The mint in the dough really adds flavor to the eggs and cheese. Basil can be substituted if desired. Serve with fresh fruit garnished with mint leaves.*

## DOUGH

¾ cup milk
2 tbs. butter or margarine
1 tbs. sugar
½ tsp. salt

1 tbs. chopped fresh mint, or 1 tsp. dried
2 cups all-purpose flour
1 tsp. yeast

## FILLING

¾ cup heavy cream
3 eggs, beaten
½ tsp. white pepper
¼ tsp. salt

1 cup ricotta cheese
½ cup grated fresh Parmesan cheese
2 oz. (½ cup ) grated Swiss cheese
2 oz. (½ cup) grated mozzarella cheese

Make dough on the dough/manual cycle of the bread machine. Upon completion of the dough cycle, roll dough into a 9-x-13-inch rectangle and place in a greased 9-x-13-inch baking dish. Prick bottom with a fork in several places, cover and let rise for about 20 minutes. While dough is rising, heat cream in a large bowl in the microwave for 1 minute or in a saucepan over medium heat until warm. Add eggs and seasonings, mix well and set aside.

Press dough into bottom and up sides of baking dish, making a rim. Mix cheeses together and spread evenly over dough. Pour cream and egg mixture over cheese and bake immediately in a preheated 350° oven for 45 to 50 minutes, or until top is brown and a toothpick inserted in the center comes out clean. If the top is browning too quickly and filling is not done, place some aluminum foil loosely on top to prevent burning.

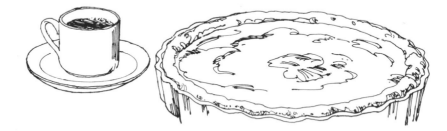

# LEMON CHEESE PIE

Servings: 6-8

*If you love lemon as much as I do, you'll love this brunch pie!*

## DOUGH
⅔ cup water
1 tbs. lemon juice
2 tbs. butter or margarine
2 tsp. dried lemon peel, or grated peel (zest) from 1 medium lemon
2 tbs. sugar
1 tsp. salt
2 cups all-purpose flour
1 tsp. yeast

## FILLING
8 oz. cream cheese, softened
1 cup ricotta cheese
1 large egg
2 tbs. sugar
2 tsp. dried lemon peel, or grated peel (zest) from 1 medium lemon
1½ tsp. lemon juice

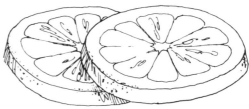

Make dough on the dough/manual cycle of the bread machine. At the same time, blend cream cheese and cottage cheese with an electric mixer. Add remaining filling ingredients and mix well until light and fluffy, about 2 to 3 minutes.

Upon completion of the dough cycle, remove 1/3 of the dough and set aside for the top crust. Roll larger piece into a 10-inch round. Place dough in a greased 9-inch deep-dish pie pan so it comes up sides of pan. Spoon filling into dough. Roll remaining dough into a rectangle. With a knife, pastry cutter or pizza cutter, cut dough into 1-inch strips and weave them across top of filling to make a lattice. Trim edges and press together with bottom crust. Bake immediately in a preheated 350° oven for about 30 minutes.

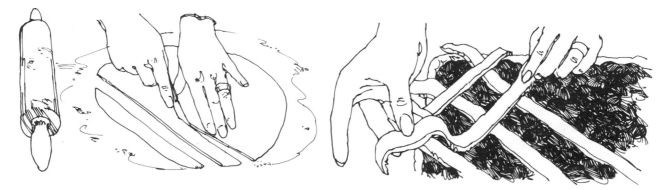

# FRUIT PIE

*This makes wonderful brunch fare, but could also be served as a dessert with vanilla ice cream or frozen yogurt on top. Prepare the dough the night before, to save time in the morning. You can also mix together the sugar, cinnamon, flour and nuts in a bowl the night before. In the morning, peel the apples and mix in the cold butter. This may also be made completely in the morning. After the dough is shaped, cover with a towel and let rise in a warm, draft-free location for about 45 minutes. If you slice the apples before the dough is ready, sprinkle a little (about a teaspoon) lemon or orange juice on them to prevent browning.*

## DOUGH
½ cup milk
1 egg
1 tbs. butter or margarine
¼ cup sugar
½ tsp. salt
2 cups all-purpose flour
1½ tsp. yeast

## TOPPING

2 medium apples
1/2 cup (1 stick) cold butter
1/2 cup sugar
1 tsp. cinnamon
1/2 cup all-purpose flour
1/2 cup finely chopped walnuts

Make dough on the dough/manual cycle of the bread machine. Upon completion of the dough cycle, roll or pat dough into a greased 9-x-13-inch baking dish, cover with plastic wrap and refrigerate overnight.

The next morning, preheat oven to 350° and remove dough from refrigerator. Peel, core and cut apples into thin slices (you need 2 1/2 to 3 cups). Press dough into bottom and up sides of baking dish, making a rim. Layer apple slices to fill crust. Cut butter into small pieces. Add remaining ingredients and blend with fingers or a pastry cutter until crumbly. Sprinkle over apple slices. Bake for about 30 minutes or until fruit is soft and crust is golden.

# PIGS IN BREAD

Yield: 12

*This is a cross between sausage in brioche and a "pigs in a blanket" theme which is usually either sausage or hot dogs in pancakes. The sausages can be cooked a day or two in advance for a less hectic morning. While the fennel is listed as optional (I omit it for the children), it really adds that extra-special flavor to the bread that adults seem to love. Cut the sausages in half and divide the dough into 24 pieces for appetizers or for a large buffet brunch table.*

**DOUGH**
1 cup milk
1 tbs. vegetable oil
2 tbs. honey
½ tsp. salt
1 tbs. fennel seed, optional
3 cups all-purpose flour
1½ tsp. yeast

**FILLING**
12 sausage links, cooked

**WASH**
1 egg, beaten with 1-2 tbs. milk or cream

Make dough on the dough/manual cycle of the bread machine. Upon completion of the dough cycle, divide dough into 12 equal pieces. Roll each piece into a small oval, just bigger than a sausage link. Wrap each piece of dough around a sausage link to completely enclose sausage. Pinch dough together tightly to seal. (I roll the dough in between the palms of my hands to help hide the seam.) Place on a greased baking sheet, brush with egg wash and bake in a preheated 350° oven for about 20 minutes.

# DINNER ENTRÉES FROM YOUR BREAD MACHINE

# SWEDISH BREAD CASSEROLE

Servings: 6-8

*Based on a Swedish recipe, this makes a great light meal with soup and/or salad, or a side dish for a ham dinner. It is easy to throw together at the last minute and is very filling. Use a good, sharp cheddar to best complement the caraway flavor.*

½ cup milk
1 egg
1-2 tbs. caraway seeds
salt and pepper to taste
4 slices *Rye Bread*, page 23, or *Caraway Bread*, page 24
2 medium potatoes, cooked whole
1 medium white onion, coarsely chopped
4 oz. (1 cup) grated sharp cheddar cheese

Mix together milk, egg, seeds and seasonings and set aside. Cut or break bread into bite-sized pieces and spread evenly in the bottom of a greased 2-quart casserole. Thinly slice potatoes and place slices on top of bread. Spread onion on top of potatoes. Pour milk mixture over all. Sprinkle with cheese. Cover and bake in a preheated 350° oven for 20 to 25 minutes. Serve warm.

# ORIENTAL CHICKEN CASSEROLE

*This makes a fantastic, casual yet elegant dinner. The dough makes good rolls too, even if you're not making the casserole!*

## ORIENTAL DOUGH

2/3 cup water
1 tbs. sesame oil
1 tsp. (1 clove) minced garlic
1 tsp. grated ginger root, or 1/4 tsp.
   ground ginger

1 tsp. sugar
1/2 tsp. salt
1/2 tsp. coarsely ground black pepper
2 cups all-purpose flour
1 tsp. yeast

## FILLING

2 cups diced cooked chicken
3 cups chicken broth or bouillon
2 tbs. soy sauce
Tabasco Sauce to taste
1/4 tsp. salt, or to taste
1/4 tsp. cayenne pepper, or to taste
1/2 cup all-purpose flour

1 can (8 oz.) sliced water chestnuts,
   drained
2-3 scallions, chopped (white and green
   part)
1 pkg. (10 oz.) frozen broccoli florets

sesame oil for brushing

Make dough on the dough/manual cycle of the bread machine. At the same time, place chicken in a greased 2-quart casserole and set aside. In a medium skillet, heat chicken broth, soy sauce, Tabasco and seasonings. Slowly stir in flour and cook over low heat, stirring frequently, until sauce thickens, about 5 minutes. Add sauce, water chestnuts, scallions and broccoli (frozen but separated) to casserole and mix everything well.

Upon completion of the dough cycle, form dough into 8 equal balls and place on top of meat mixture (7 around the perimeter and 1 in the center). Brush top of dough with sesame oil, cover and let rise for about 30 minutes. Bake in a preheated 350° oven for about 30 minutes.

**TIP:** If you do not have leftover chicken, cut 4 boneless, skinless chicken breast halves into bite-sized pieces and sauté them in 1 to 2 tbs. sesame oil.

# WEST AFRICAN BEEF CASSEROLE

Servings: 4-6

*Based on a traditional recipe for stew, this has been modified to a casserole version. It reminds me in some ways of Indonesian satay, so I combined it with a coconut ginger dough. The meat cooks for 1 hour during the dough cycle and the 30-minute rise that follows, so start the dough about 1 hour before you cook the meat if your dough cycle takes 1½ hours, or time accordingly. A 13.5 oz. can of unsweetened coconut milk is enough for both the dough and the filling.*

## COCONUT GINGER DOUGH

7/8 cup unsweetened coconut milk
2 tbs. butter
1 tsp. grated ginger root, or ¼ tsp.
    ground ginger

1 tbs. sugar
½ tsp. salt
2 cups all-purpose flour
1 tsp. yeast

## WEST AFRICAN BEEF FILLING

¼ cup smooth peanut butter
2 cups beef bouillon
½ cup unsweetened coconut milk
1 lb. boneless stewing beef, cut into
    cubes

2 tbs. butter or margarine
¼-½ medium onion, diced
2 tbs. all-purpose flour
1 tbs. curry powder

Make dough on the dough/manual cycle of the bread machine.

Blend peanut butter, bouillon and coconut milk with a blender or food processor and set aside. In a large skillet, brown meat in butter. Remove meat from pan using a slotted spoon and set aside in a greased 2-quart casserole. Cook onion in the same butter and meat drippings until just golden in color; remove onion with a slotted spoon and add to meat. Stir curry and flour into drippings in skillet and add peanut butter-coconut milk mixture. Stir constantly over low heat until sauce has thickened, about 5 minutes. Pour mixture over meat and onions; stir briefly to mix. Bake in a preheated 350° oven for 1 hour.

Upon completion of the dough cycle, form dough into 8 equal balls. Place on a greased baking sheet to rise for about 30 minutes. Gently place risen dough balls on top of casserole. Return casserole to oven to bake for 20 minutes or until bread rolls are golden.

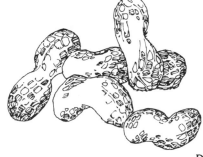

# MEAT GALETTE

Servings: 6

*This is a dream come true for leftovers. With roots in France, galettes are a cross between pizza and tarts and can be plain or stuffed with sweet fruits or savory meats and cheeses. The dough can be either a pastry dough or a yeast dough which is richer than a pizza dough. Unlike tarts, galettes are free-formed and use only the dough, and not the pan, to support the filling. Galettes may be made into one large pie or, as I prefer for meals, into smaller, individual rounds. The high egg and butter content which provides much of the liquid for this dough will result in a low rising dough. It may be necessary to add a tablespoon or two more flour to get the dough to form a ball, but be careful to not add too much — the dough should be soft and slightly sticky.*

## BASIC GALETTE DOUGH

½ cup milk
1 egg
2 tbs. butter or margarine
¼ cup sugar
½ tsp. salt
2 cups all-purpose flour
2 tsp. yeast

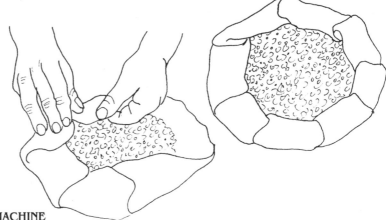

## FILLING

1½-2 cups finely diced cooked chicken, turkey, lamb or beef
4 oz. (1 cup) crumbled feta cheese
1 cup ricotta cheese

1 egg
½ tsp. salt, or to taste
½-1 tsp. pepper, to taste

## WASH

1 egg beaten with 2 tbs. milk or cream, or cream only, or olive oil or melted butter

Make dough on the dough/manual cycle of the bread machine. At the same time, mix filling ingredients together and set aside. Upon completion of the dough cycle, divide dough into 6 equal pieces. Roll each piece into a 6-inch round and place about ½ cup of the filling in the center, leaving a 2-inch border. Fold one section of the border dough over to cover the outer edge of the filling and repeat process all around outer edge of galette, pleating dough. The center of the galette will not be covered. Brush dough top with wash to make a glossy sheen to the finished product. Bake immediately in a preheated 350° oven for about 20 minutes. Serve warm.

# MEXICAN PIE

*Use your favorite salsa, hot and spicy, medium or mild. Serve the pie with sour cream if desired. If you're making it for finicky kids, you can omit the jalapeños in the dough.*

## DOUGH

⅔ cup water
2 tbs. vegetable or canola oil
½-1 jalapeño pepper, diced, optional
1 tbs. sugar
½ tsp. salt

½ cup masa harina or cornmeal
1½ cups all-purpose flour
1½ tsp. yeast

## FILLING

1 lb. ground beef or turkey
¼ cup chopped onion
1 tsp. (2 cloves) minced garlic
½-1 jalapeño pepper, diced

1 tsp. ground cumin
2 tsp. paprika
1 cup salsa
4 oz. (1 cup) grated cheddar cheese

Make dough on the dough/manual cycle of the bread machine. At the same time, mix together meat, onion, garlic, jalapeño, cumin and paprika until well blended. Cook meat mixture in a large skillet over medium heat until meat is well browned and onions are tender; drain any fat and remove from heat; set aside to cool.

Upon completion of the dough cycle, remove dough and roll on a lightly floured surface into a 10- to 11-inch round. Place dough in the bottom and up the sides of a greased 9-inch pie pan. Spoon meat mixture evenly into dough. Spread salsa over meat and sprinkle evenly with cheese. Bake immediately or cover loosely with plastic and refrigerate for 2 to 3 hours. Bake in a preheated 350° oven for about 30 minutes.

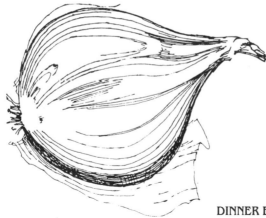

# EASY CHICKEN POT PIE

Servings: 6-8

*This is a very simple, throw-together pot pie. Select your favorite filling.*

## DOUGH

⅞ cup milk
2 tbs. butter or margarine
½ tsp. salt

1 tsp. dried parsley, or 1 tbs. chopped
   fresh
2 cups bread flour
1 tsp. yeast

## CHICKEN AND VEGETABLE FILLING

1½-2 cups diced cooked chicken or
   turkey
1 pkg. (10 oz.) frozen mixed vegetables
¼ cup milk

1 can (10¾ oz.) cream of chicken soup
1 tsp. coarsely ground pepper, or to taste
1 tsp. dried parsley, or 1 tbs. chopped
   fresh

## CHICKEN, BROCCOLI AND CHEESE FILLING

1-1½ cups diced cooked chicken or
   turkey
1 pkg. (10 oz.) frozen chopped broccoli
4 oz. (1 cup) grated cheddar cheese
¼ cup milk

1 can (10¾ oz.) cream of broccoli soup
1 tsp. coarsely ground pepper, or to
   taste
1 tsp. dried parsley, or 1 tbs. chopped
   fresh

## WASH
1 egg beaten with 2 tbs. milk or cream, or milk or cream only

Make dough on the dough/manual cycle of the bread machine. Upon completion of the dough cycle, remove 1/3 of the dough and set aside for the top crust. Roll larger piece into a 10-inch round and place in a greased, 9-inch deep dish pie pan. The dough will come up the sides of the pan.

Place chicken and vegetables (and cheese for second filling) in the center of dough. Stir milk into soup to thin; add seasoning. Pour soup over chicken and vegetables. Roll remaining dough into a 9-inch round and cover filling. Fold bottom crust over top crust and press edges together with fingers to seal tightly. Brush top of dough with a wash. Pierce top with a fork or knife in several places to allow steam to vent. Bake immediately in a preheated 350° oven for about 35 minutes.

# SHEPHERD'S PIE

*Traditionally this dish is served with mashed potatoes on top. Here's a variation that uses potato bread in a dumpling fashion on top of the pie instead.*

## POTATO PARSLEY DOUGH

⅞ cup milk
2 tbs. butter
½ tsp. salt
1 tbs. chopped fresh parsley, or
    1 tsp. dried

½ cup instant potato flakes
2 cups all-purpose flour
1½ tsp. yeast

## SHEPHERD'S PIE FILLING

3 tbs. butter or margarine
¼ cup diced onion
1 stalk celery, diced
2 cups diced cooked beef or lamb

1½ cups sliced mushrooms
2 tbs. flour
salt and pepper to taste
3 cups beef bouillon

Make dough on the dough/manual cycle of the bread machine. At the same time, melt ½ of the butter in a large skillet over medium heat. Cook onion and celery until soft, about 4 to 5 minutes. Using a slotted spoon, remove vegetables and place in a greased 2-quart casserole with meat. Sauté mushrooms in the same butter until just soft, 1 to 2 minutes, and transfer to casserole. Melt remaining butter in skillet and, using a fork or whisk, slowly stir in flour until well blended. Add seasonings and stir in bouillon or broth. Stir over medium heat until mixture thickens, about 3 to 4 minutes. Pour liquid over meat mixture in casserole and set aside.

Upon completion of the dough cycle, remove dough and form into 8 equal balls. Place balls on top of meat mixture, cover and let rise for about 20 to 30 minutes. Bake in a preheated 350° oven for about 20 minutes or until bread is golden brown. Spoon filling on individual plates and serve with a piece of bread topping.

**TIP:** If you do not have leftover meat, brown 1 lb. beef stew cubes (lean round steak) in 1 tbs. butter. Remove meat with a slotted spoon and place in a greased 2-quart casserole. Continue with recipe as before until all ingredients are in casserole. Bake meat mixture, covered, for about 1 hour. Let bread balls rise on a greased baking sheet for 20 to 30 minutes while meat is baking. Remove casserole from oven and gently place bread balls on top of hot meat mixture. Return casserole to oven and bake, uncovered, for 20 minutes or until bread is golden brown.

# INDIAN PIE

*The seasonings in this dish are used frequently in Middle Eastern and West Indian cuisine. If using ground turkey, this makes an easy low fat meal with a salad.*

## GINGER DOUGH

⅔ cup water
1 tbs. olive or vegetable oil
1 tsp. sugar
½ tsp. salt
1 tsp. (2 cloves) minced garlic

1 tsp. minced ginger root, or ¼ tsp.
    ground ginger
2 cups all-purpose flour
1 tsp. yeast

## INDIAN FILLING

1 lb. ground turkey, lamb or beef
¼ cup diced onion
1 tsp. (2 cloves) minced garlic
½ tsp. ground coriander
¼ tsp. ground cumin
1 tsp. minced ginger root, or ¼ tsp.
    ground ginger

¼ tsp. salt, or to taste
½ tsp. pepper, or to taste
1 egg
1 cup cottage cheese
¼ cup chopped cilantro or fresh
    parsley, or 1 tbs. dried

Make dough on the dough/manual cycle of the bread machine. At the same time, cook meat, onion and garlic in a large skillet until meat is browned and onion is soft. Add seasonings and remove from heat. Beat egg, blend with cottage cheese and set aside.

Upon completion of the dough cycle, remove dough and roll into a 10- to 11-inch round. Place in a greased 9-inch pie pan so dough comes up the sides. Spoon meat mixture over dough, spread with cottage cheese-egg mixture and sprinkle with cilantro or parsley. Bake immediately or cover and place in the refrigerator for 2 to 3 hours. Bake uncovered in a preheated 350° oven for about 30 minutes.

# HAM IN A RYE CRUST

Servings: 12+

*Ham and rye go hand in hand in this beautifully presented ham dinner. It's important to use a fully cooked ham so that it only needs to be warmed while the dough is baking around it. A boneless ham will be easier to serve.*

## DOUGH

7/8 cup water
3 tbs. vegetable oil
2 tbs. molasses
1/2 tsp. salt
1 tbs. unsweetened cocoa powder

1 tsp. dried onion flakes
1 tbs. caraway seeds, optional
1 1/2 cups rye flour
1 1/2 cups bread flour
2 tsp. yeast

## FILLING

1/2 medium onion, thinly sliced, optional
1 fully cooked, boneless ham, about 5 lb., round or oval

vegetable oil for brushing

Make dough on the dough/manual cycle of the bread machine. Upon completion of the dough cycle, remove dough and roll it into a large rectangle on a lightly floured surface. Spread onion, if using, on the dough, leaving a 1-inch border on all sides. Place ham in center of dough and wrap dough around ham. Pinch closed with fingers. Place dough-wrapped ham, seam-side up, on a greased perforated pizza pan, cover with a towel and let rise in a warm, draft-free location for about 30 minutes. Brush dough with vegetable oil and bake in a preheated 350° oven for about 45 minutes. Cool on a wire rack for 10 minutes before cutting into ½-inch slices to serve.

# MEAT LOAF IN BRIOCHE

Servings: 4-6

*Nothing will dress up your favorite meat loaf more than wrapping it in a brioche dough. This meat loaf recipe, loaded with cheese, is my favorite. Another recipe of the same size will also work.*

## CHEESY MEAT LOAF

2 slices *Garlic Parsley* Bread, page 29,
 or *Garlic Basil Bread*, page 28, or
 leftover plain or herb bread
1 lb. ground beef or turkey
4 oz. (1 cup) grated cheddar cheese
1 egg

1 cup milk
1/4 cup chopped onion
1/2 tsp. salt
1/2 tsp. pepper
1 tsp. dried parsley or basil (to match
 bread)

Remove crusts from bread and process with a food processor until finely chopped into soft crumbs (should be about 1 cup of crumbs). Combine with all other meat loaf ingredients, mixing well. Place mixture in a greased 5-x-9-inch meat loaf pan and bake, uncovered, in a preheated 350° oven for 1 hour. Remove meat loaf from pan and cool on a wire rack for about 1 hour (while dough is in the machine). If desired, cook meat loaf a day in advance, wrap in aluminum foil and refrigerate until ready to enclose with dough and bake.

## BRIOCHE DOUGH

½ cup milk
2 tbs. butter
2 eggs
2 tbs. sugar

1 tsp. salt
2½ cups all-purpose flour
2 tsp. yeast

## WASH

1 egg beaten with 1 tbs. water, or cream only

Make dough on the dough/manual cycle of the bread machine. Upon completion of the dough cycle, remove dough to a lightly floured surface. Dough may be slightly sticky, but add only enough flour to work dough without sticking. Roll into a large rectangle and place cooked meat loaf in the center. Wrap dough around meat loaf and pinch seam with fingers to seal. Place loaf on a greased baking sheet, cover and let rise for about 45 minutes. Brush with egg wash or cream and pierce dough in several places for steam to escape. Bake in a preheated 350° oven for 25 to 30 minutes. Cut into 1-inch slices to serve.

## SAUSAGE IN BRIOCHE

Substitute a sausage (about 1½ lb., 4-8 inches long and 2-3½ inches in diameter) for meat loaf. Follow directions for *Meat Loaf in Brioche*, but bake for 30 to 35 minutes. Slice into ½-inch slices for appetizers or 1-inch slices for a light meal with a salad and/or soup.

# BEEF WELLINGTON

Servings: 10-12

*Traditionally a rich, buttery pastry dough is used for Beef Wellington. This variation uses an herb-flavored yeast dough for fewer calories and lots of flavor. Duxelles is a flavoring paste, traditionally made from mushrooms, shallots and herbs cooked in butter. This version has bell peppers to add flavor and color and can be made in advance.*

## DUXELLES

8 oz. mushrooms
1 red bell pepper, chopped
1 green bell pepper, chopped
1/4 cup chopped onion
2 tbs. chopped fresh parsley

1/4 cup beef broth or bouillon
2 tbs. Madeira wine
1/2 tsp. dried thyme
salt and pepper to taste

Process mushrooms, bell peppers, onion and parsley with a food processor until finely chopped and blended. Place vegetable mixture in a medium saucepan with beef broth and Madeira and bring to a boil. Reduce heat to medium high, add thyme, salt and pepper and cook until liquid starts to thicken, about 10 minutes. Reduce heat and simmer for about 30 minutes, stirring frequently; do not allow to scorch. Remove from heat and cool completely. This can be made in advance and refrigerated.

## THYME DOUGH

2/3 cup water
2 tbs. olive oil
1 tsp. (2 cloves) minced garlic
1/2 tsp. salt

2 tbs. fresh thyme, or 2 tsp. dried,
  crushed
2 cups all-purpose flour
1 tsp. yeast

## WASH

1 egg white beaten with 1 tbs. water

2 1/2-3 lb. beef tenderloin roast
1 tbs. butter, optional

Make dough on the dough/manual cycle of the bread machine. When cycle begins (if 1 1/2-hour cycle), trim excess fat from meat. Sear in 1 tbs. butter or in a large nonstick skillet over medium heat. Transfer meat to a plate and allow to cool for about 1 hour. Upon completion of the dough cycle, roll dough on a lightly floured surface into a rectangle, just slightly longer than meat (not too wide or thin as dough may tear). Spread cold *Duxelles* over meat to completely cover all surfaces. Fold dough to completely encase meat. Pinch seams tightly closed. Place on a greased baking sheet and brush with egg white wash. Bake in a preheated 375° oven for 50 to 60 minutes or until center of meat is registers 150° on a meat thermometer (for medium). Slice meat with a serrated knife and serve with warm *Madeira Sauce* (please turn the page).

## MADEIRA SAUCE

1 cup beef broth
1 cup Madeira wine
1 medium tomato, finely chopped
¼ cup finely chopped onion

1 tsp. (2 cloves) minced garlic
¼ tsp. thyme
1 tbs. cornstarch
1 tbs. water

In a medium saucepan, combine broth, Madeira, tomato, onion, garlic and thyme; bring to a boil. Reduce heat to low and simmer for about 25 minutes. Strain mixture through a cheesecloth-lined colander and return strained liquid to pan. Using a fork or small whisk, mix cornstarch and water and add slowly to liquid, stirring constantly until well blended. Simmer over low heat until mixture has thickened, about 2 to 3 minutes. Sauce can be rewarmed to serve.

# PORK TENDERLOIN
# WITH APRICOT STUFFING

*This stuffing recipe can also be used for a 4 or 5 lb. chicken, or tripled for an 18-20 lb. turkey. Apricot fruit spread is sold with jams and jellies.*

## APRICOT STUFFING

5 cups cubed *Apricot Bread*, page 16
   (about 5-6 slices), lightly packed
2 tbs. butter or margarine, melted
1 egg
$3/4$ cup orange juice

$1/2$ tsp. salt
1 tsp. pepper
$1/4$ cup chopped walnuts
5-6 dried apricots, diced

Combine all ingredients and mix until just blended.

2 pork tenderloins, $3/4$ lb. each

1 tbs. apricot fruit spread

Make a lengthwise cut about $3/4$ of the way through the middle of each tenderloin. Fill each cavity with $1/2$ of the stuffing. Tie tenderloins with kitchen string to close. Spread $1/2$ of the apricot fruit spread over each tenderloin. Spray the top of a broiler pan with nonstick cooking spray and fill bottom section with about $1/2$-inch of water. Roast tenderloins on pan in a preheated 325° oven for about 35 to 45 minutes.

# ROAST CHICKEN WITH
# SAUSAGE OR CRANBERRY STUFFING

Servings: 4-6

*These recipes make about 3 cups of stuffing or enough for a 7 to 10 lb. bird, and can easily be doubled or tripled for larger birds (triple for a 20 lb. turkey). Bring the stuffing to room temperature before you fill the bird, and roast the bird immediately after stuffing. Bake extra stuffing in a covered casserole at the same time.*

1 roasting chicken, 4-5 lb.
olive oil for rubbing
salt and pepper to taste

Stuff chicken cavity loosely with *Sausage* or *Cranberry Stuffing*. Line a roasting pan with 2 sheets of heavy-duty aluminum foil, leaving enough foil hanging over the sides to wrap bird completely. Rub outside of chicken with olive oil and sprinkle with salt and pepper. Place bird breast side down in pan and wrap tightly with foil. Roast in a preheated 350° oven for 25 minutes per pound. About 15 to 20 minutes before the end of the roasting period, unwrap bird and turn breast side up to brown.

## SAUSAGE STUFFING

1/4-1/2 medium onion, chopped
1/2 lb. sausage, cooked, drained and
   crumbled
1-2 stalks celery, diced

5 cups cubed *Caraway Bread*, page 24,
   made with fennel instead of caraway
   (about 5-6 slices), lightly packed
1 egg
3/4 cup water or chicken stock

Cook onion and sausage in a large skillet until meat is brown and onion is soft. Remove from heat and drain well. Combine with remaining ingredients and mix until just blended. Stuff bird loosely and roast as directed.

## CRANBERRY STUFFING

1/2-1 medium onion, diced
2 tbs. butter or margarine
1 egg
3/4 cup orange juice
1/2 tsp. salt
1 tsp. pepper

1/4 cup sliced or chopped almonds
1/2 cup fresh cranberries
5 cups crumbled *Fruit Bread*, page 15,
   *Apple Cinnamon Raisin Bread*, page 21,
   or *Cranberry Nut Bread*, page 22
   (about 5-6 slices), lightly packed

Cook onion in butter until just soft and starting to brown. Combine with remaining ingredients and mix until just blended. Stuff bird cavity loosely and roast as directed.

# HERB-STUFFED CHICKEN BREASTS

Servings: 4

*This is incredibly easy and is perfect for a casual, yet elegant meal. Serve with cranberry sauce and you'll think it's Thanksgiving!*

3 tbs. butter
1/4 cup finely chopped onion
1 tsp. (2 cloves) minced garlic
1 1/2 cups cubed *Garlic Parsley Bread*, page 29, or *Garlic Basil Bread*, page 28
1 egg

1/4 tsp. salt
1/2 tsp. pepper
2 tsp. dried parsley or basil (depending on bread used), or 2 tbs. chopped fresh
4 boneless, skinless chicken breast halves

Heat 1 tbs. of the butter in a medium skillet and cook onion and garlic until just tender, about 5 minutes. Remove skillet from heat and cool slightly. Combine mixture with bread, egg, salt, pepper and 1/2 of the herbs in a large bowl, mixing well. Place 1/4 of the stuffing in the center of each breast half. Fold edges together to encase stuffing, using a toothpick to hold chicken meat closed if desired. Place seam side down in a greased 8-inch square baking dish. Melt remaining 2 tbs. butter and combine with remaining herbs. Brush top of chicken with herb butter and bake uncovered in a preheated 350° oven for about 30 minutes.

# HERB-STUFFED BEEF TENDERLOIN

Servings: 10-12

*This easy, elegant meal will impress your guests.*

## STUFFING

2 cups cubed *Garlic Parsley Bread*,
    page 26, or *Garlic Basil Bread*, page
    25, or leftover herb bread
1/4 cup chopped walnuts
1/4 cup butter or margarine

1 egg
1/4 tsp. salt
1/2 tsp. pepper
1 tsp. dried parsley or basil (depending
    on bread used), or 1 tbs. chopped fresh

Place bread cubes in a medium bowl. In a small skillet, brown nuts in butter over low heat, about 1 minute. Add butter and nuts to bread, mixing well. Add egg, salt, pepper and herb and mix until well blended.

1 beef tenderloin, 2 1/2-3 lb., trimmed
4 slices bacon

Make a lengthwise cut about 3/4 of the way through the middle of the meat. Place stuffing in cavity. Wrap bacon around meat to help hold it closed over stuffing and fasten together with toothpicks. Place tenderloin in a greased 9-x-13-inch baking dish. Bake uncovered in a preheated 350° oven for 50 to 60 minutes.

# HOMEMADE PASTA WITH FRESH VEGETABLES   Servings: 2

*Your bread machine makes wonderful pasta dough. Once the dough is made, simply roll it out, cut it and cook it. The best flour for pasta is milled from durum wheat and is generally found in the flour or specialty section of the grocery store labeled "semolina or pasta flour." If you find that you enjoy the fresh pasta, it is worth investing in a hand-cranked pasta machine (under $50) to roll and cut the dough very thinly. For more tips and more than 100 pasta recipes for your bread machine and a hand-cranked machine, see my book, **THE PASTA MACHINE COOKBOOK.** Use steamed vegetables for a great low fat topping.*

### BASIC PASTA DOUGH                              Yield: about 8 oz. fresh pasta
1 cup semolina (pasta) flour
1 large egg
1 tbs. olive oil
up to 1 tbs. water (only) if needed

Place ingredients in the bread machine in the order given. It does not matter which cycle you use. Allow the machine to knead the dough for a minute or so until a dough ball has been formed. Check the consistency and add flour or water if necessary to form a round ball of dough. Dough will be heavier than a bread dough but it should be smooth. Allow the machine to knead the dough for about 5 minutes and then turn the machine off. Leave dough in machine for 10 to 15 minutes. Lightly flour dough and roll through a hand-cranked pasta machine, following manufacturer's directions for the machine. If you do not have a hand-cranked pasta machine, divide dough into quarters and roll each quarter into a rectangle as large and as thin as possible. Using a pastry knife or pizza wheel, cut pasta dough into long fettuccine-sized strips. If dough becomes sticky as you roll it, sprinkle with a little more semolina flour. Cook pasta immediately in 2 to 3 quarts boiling water, stirring it as soon as it hits the water to avoid clumping. Fresh pasta cooks in 1 to 2 minutes and is done when it is tender but still firm to the bite (*al dente*). Serve immediately with *Steamed Vegetable Topping*.

## STEAMED VEGETABLE TOPPING
1 tbs. full-flavored olive oil
2-4 cups vegetables (sliced carrots, broccoli, cauliflower, snow peas, etc.), steamed
salt and pepper to taste
¼ cup freshly grated Parmesan cheese

Toss pasta with olive oil and steamed vegetables. Season and sprinkle with Parmesan. Serve immediately on warm plates.

# DESSERTS FROM YOUR BREAD MACHINE

# TRADITIONAL BREAD PUDDING

Servings: 8

*Puddings are a terrific way to use up leftovers, whether rice or bread. In most bread pudding recipes, the bread is buttered. I find, however, that if the bread is soaked completely in the milk, the butter (and resulting extra calories) is unnecessary.*

4 slices *Cranberry Nut bread*, page 22,
    *Apple Cinnamon Raisin Bread*, page 21,
    *Fruit Bread*, page 15, *Lemon Bread*,
    page 16, *Orange Bread*, page 17; or
    any leftover sweet bread
1/2 cup raisins

3 cups milk
1/3 cup sugar
4 eggs
1 tsp. vanilla or other flavor extract
cinnamon to taste

Cut or break bread into bite-sized pieces and place in a buttered 8-inch square baking pan; sprinkle with raisins. Bring milk to a boil, remove from heat and stir in sugar until dissolved; set aside to cool slightly. Beat eggs and slowly add to milk, stirring constantly. Stir in vanilla extract. Pour egg-milk mixture over bread and sprinkle with cinnamon. Place baking pan in a larger baking pan and fill the larger pan with hot water to come about halfway up sides of smaller pan. Bake in a preheated 350° oven for about 45 to 50 minutes, until a knife inserted in the center comes out clean. Serve warm.

# TROPICAL BREAD PUDDING

*I use "light" fruit cocktail for this delightful dessert. Sprinkle shredded coconut on top with the nuts for a variation.*

4 slices *Hawaiian Bread*, page 18,
    *Lemon Bread*, page 16, *Orange
    Bread*, page 17, or any leftover sweet
    fruited bread
1 cup milk
¼ cup brown sugar, firmly packed

1 can (15 oz.) fruit cocktail with juice
4 eggs
1 tsp. vanilla extract
cinnamon to taste
¼ cup finely ground nuts (walnuts,
    pecans or almonds)

Cut or break bread into bite-sized pieces and place in a buttered 8-inch square baking pan. Bring milk to a boil, remove from heat and stir in sugar and fruit cocktail with juice. Beat eggs and slowly add to milk, stirring constantly; stir in vanilla. Pour egg-milk mixture over bread and sprinkle with cinnamon and ground nuts. Place baking pan in a larger baking pan and fill the larger pan with hot water to come about halfway up sides of smaller pan. Bake in a preheated 350° oven for about 40 to 50 minutes, or until a knife inserted in the center comes out clean. Serve warm.

# PIÑA COLADA BREAD PUDDING

Servings: 8

*This is out of this world for dessert, or even a decadent breakfast.*

4 slices *Hawaiian Bread*, page 18, *Coconut Bread*, page 20, *Lemon Bread*, page 16,
   or any leftover sweet bread
1 cup milk
1 can (15-16 oz.) frozen piña colada mix concentrate, thawed
4 eggs, beaten
1 tsp. coconut extract
2-3 tbs. shredded coconut

Cut or break bread into bite-sized pieces and place in a buttered 8-inch square baking pan. Bring milk to a boil, remove from heat and stir in piña colada mix, eggs and coconut extract. Pour egg-milk mixture over bread and sprinkle with shredded coconut. Place baking pan in a larger baking pan and fill the larger pan with hot water to come about halfway up sides of smaller pan. Bake in a preheated 350° oven for about 40 to 50 minutes, or until a knife inserted in the center comes out clean. Serve warm.

# MEXICAN CAPRIOTADA

Servings: 8

*Similar to a bread pudding, this is traditionally eaten only at Easter.*

3 cups water
two 2-inch cinnamon sticks
1/2 cup raisins
1/2 cup sugar
6 thick slices *Lemon Bread*, page 16, *Orange Bread*, page 17, or any leftover sweet
    bread
8 oz. (2 cups) shredded cheddar cheese

In a medium saucepan, heat water over medium low heat with cinnamon sticks and raisins until water is hot and golden in color, about 15 minutes. Stir in sugar, stirring constantly until it dissolves. Discard cinnamon sticks, remove from heat and allow to cool. Cut or break bread into bite-sized pieces. Spread 1/2 of the bread in a buttered 2-quart deep casserole and pour 1/2 of the liquid mixture on top to soak bread. Layer with 1 cup of the cheddar cheese. Repeat layers in the same order. Place casserole in a larger baking pan and fill larger pan with hot water to come about halfway up sides of casserole. Bake in a preheated 350° oven for about 20 to 30 minutes, or until a knife inserted in the center comes out clean. Serve warm.

# STRAWBERRY PUDDING

*This is a perfect solution for leftover sweet bread and fresh strawberries. Don't even think of using frozen strawberries in this, as it will be too soggy. Serve with whipped cream, vanilla ice cream or frozen yogurt.*

1 qt. fresh strawberries, hulled and sliced
1/4 cup all-purpose flour
1 cup milk
2 slices *Orange Bread*, page 17, *Coconut Bread*,
    page 20, or any leftover sweet bread
1/4 cup sugar
2 tbs. butter

Sprinkle strawberries with flour and set aside for about 30 minutes. Cut or break bread into bite-sized pieces and place in a greased 2-quart casserole. Heat milk for about 3 minutes or until hot. Pour milk over bread, sprinkle with sugar and spread berries on top. Cut butter into small pieces and dot berries with butter. Bake uncovered in a preheated 350° oven for about 45 minutes. Serve warm.

# PEACH BETTY

*With roots in the American colonies, betties are made with layers of fruits and breadcrumbs. You could say betties are a cross between bread puddings and cobblers (which use a pastry topping). This is an easy, elegant dessert using any sweet leftover bread. It's good served with vanilla ice cream or yogurt.*

4 slices *Apricot Bread*, page 19, *Lemon Bread*, page 16, or any leftover sweet bread
1/4 cup butter or margarine, melted

3 cups sliced fresh peaches, or 1 can (29 oz.) sliced peaches, drained
1 cup sweetened lemonade
1 tsp. cinnamon or nutmeg

Break bread into pieces and process with a food processor or blender to make crumbs. Mix crumbs with melted butter to soften. Layer 1/3 of the crumbs in the bottom of a buttered 2-quart casserole. Place 1/2 of the peaches on top of crumbs. Pour 1/2 of the lemonade over peaches and sprinkle with 1/2 of the cinnamon. Place another 1/3 of the crumbs on top of the peaches, layer with remaining peaches and pour over remaining lemonade. Top with remaining crumbs. Cover and bake in a preheated 325° oven for about 1 hour. Serve warm.

**TIP:** To make lemonade, mix 1/2 cup water, 3 tbs. fresh lemon juice and about 3/4 cup sugar.

# APPLE RAISIN BETTY

Servings: 8

*This is a wonderful fall treat. As a variation to the cinnamon, try using either apple or pumpkin pie spice. Serve with vanilla ice cream or yogurt.*

4 slices *Apple Cinnamon Raisin Bread*, page 21, or any leftover sweet bread
1/4 cup butter or margarine, melted
3 cups sliced peeled apples (2 1/2-3 apples)
1 tbs. lemon juice
1/2 cup raisins or craisins
1/2 cup sweetened apple juice
2 tsp. cinnamon

Break bread into pieces and process with a food processor or blender to make crumbs. Toss with melted butter to soften. Press 1/3 of the crumbs in the bottom of a buttered 2-quart casserole. Immediately toss sliced apples with lemon juice to prevent browning. Place 1/2 of the apples and 1/2 of the raisins on top of crumbs. Pour 1/2 of the apple juice over apples and sprinkle with 1 tsp. of the cinnamon. Repeat layering, ending with remaining 1/3 of the breadcrumbs. With your hands, press down on crumbs to compact and soak with liquid. Cover and bake in a preheated 350° oven for about 45 minutes. Serve warm.

# APPLE CHARLOTTE

*This is so quick and easy, it is unbelievable! It's like having an apple pie without any of the hassle. You can break the bread into bite-sized pieces instead of using slices, and toss the pieces with the butter.*

6-7 slices *Apple Cinnamon Raisin Bread*, page 21
1/4 cup butter, melted
1 can (20 or 21 oz.) apple pie filling
1/2 cup chopped almonds or walnuts

Remove crusts from bread. Brush each slice of bread with melted butter. Place 1/2 of the slices on the bottom of a greased 8-inch baking dish. Pour apple filling on top of buttered bread and sprinkle with nuts. Cover with remaining bread and drizzle with any remaining butter. Bake in a preheated 350° oven for about 30 minutes. Serve warm.

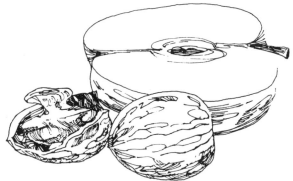

# EASY CREAM LAYERED CAKE

Servings: 8

*While this may appear complicated, once you have made one, you'll realize that it is quite easy and a great use for leftover sweet breads. The easiest of the layered cakes in this chapter, this one uses a simple flavored whipped cream for the filling. Serve topped with additional whipped cream or vanilla ice cream and nuts.*

1 pt. heavy whipping cream, chilled
1/2 cup confectioners' sugar
8-10 slices *Cranberry Nut Bread*, page 22, *Apple Cinnamon Raisin Bread*, page 21,
 *French Walnut Bread*, page 23, or any leftover sweet bread
1/4 cup chopped walnuts, pecans or almonds (to match nut in bread)

Beat whipping cream and confectioners' sugar together until stiff. Set aside. Remove crusts from bread. Cut each slice of bread into 4 equal rectangles. Press enough rectangles into a greased, floured 9-inch springform pan to completely cover bottom. Bread can be cut to fit as necessary. Set remaining bread aside.

Spread whipped cream filling evenly on top of bread. Layer remaining bread rectangles on top, arranged like spokes of a wheel.

Cover with aluminum foil and weigh down with a plate. Chill overnight or for a minimum of 8 hours. Remove sides of springform pan and serve sprinkled with nuts.

# LAYERED CHOCOLATE COCONUT CAKE

Servings: 8

*Serve topped with whipped cream or ice cream, sprinkled with coconut and/or chocolate sprinkles or chips. Guests will marvel.*

9-11 slices *Coconut Bread*, page 20
4 eggs, separated
2 oz. (2 squares) unsweetened chocolate
$\frac{1}{2}$ cup granulated sugar
$\frac{1}{4}$ cup water
1 cup butter or margarine, softened
1 cup confectioners' sugar
1 tsp. coconut extract
$\frac{1}{2}$ cup sweetened shredded coconut

Remove crusts from bread. Cut each slice into 4 equal rectangles. Press enough rectangles into a greased, floured 9-inch springform pan to completely cover bottom. Bread can be cut to fit as necessary. Set remaining bread aside.

Beat egg yolks and set aside. Beat egg whites until stiff peaks form and set aside. In the top of a double boiler, melt chocolate. Add granulated sugar and stir constantly until sugar is dissolved; stir in water. Add egg yolks, stirring constantly, and cook until smooth and thick, about 2 minutes. Remove from heat and cool slightly. Cream butter and confectioners' sugar. Add coconut extract, shredded coconut and chocolate-egg yolk mixture, stirring to combine. Fold in egg whites.

Layer 1/2 of the chocolate filling on top of bread, spreading evenly. Repeat layers of bread and filling, ending with bread rectangles on top, arranged like spokes of a wheel.

Cover with aluminum foil and weigh down with a plate. Chill overnight or for a minimum of 8 hours. Remove sides of springform pan and serve.

# LEMON LAYERED CAKE

Servings: 8

*This is a perfect dessert for guests, because it must be made a day in advance. Serve topped with whipped cream or ice cream, sprinkled with almond slices.*

1 tbs. cornstarch
¼ cup milk
3 eggs, separated
¼ cup granulated sugar
juice of 1 large lemon, or 3 tbs. lemon juice
1 tsp. dried or grated fresh lemon peel (zest), or to taste
4 oz. cream cheese, softened
1 cup confectioners' sugar
½ cup sliced almonds
8-10 slices *Lemon Bread*, page 16

Mix cornstarch into milk and set aside. Beat egg yolks and transfer to the top of a double boiler with granulated sugar and cornstarch-milk mixture. Cook until smooth and thick (3 to 4 minutes), stirring constantly. Remove from heat, add juice and peel or zest and allow to cool. Cream cream cheese and confectioners' sugar and add to milk mixture. Fold in almonds. Beat egg whites until stiff peaks form and fold into filling.

Remove crusts from bread. Cut each slice of bread into 4 equal rectangles. Press enough rectangles into a greased, floured 9-inch springform pan to completely cover bottom. Bread can be cut to fit as necessary. Set remaining bread aside.

Layer 1/2 of the filling on top of bread, spreading evenly. Repeat layers of bread and filling, ending with bread rectangles on top, arranged like spokes of a wheel. Cover with aluminum foil and weigh down with a plate. Chill overnight or for a minimum of 8 hours. Remove sides of springform pan and serve.

# STRAWBERRY KUCHEN

Servings: 12

*Fruit kuchens (German) are fruit- or cheese-filled cakes which use a sweet, yeast-leavened dough instead of a pastry base. In this version, the fruit is covered with a custard mixture. Enjoy this as a dessert, or with coffee for breakfast or brunch. Serve with whipped cream, vanilla ice cream or yogurt.*

## DOUGH
¾ cup milk
1 egg
¼ cup butter
⅓ cup sugar
1 tsp. salt
¼ tsp. nutmeg
3 cups all-purpose flour
2 tsp. yeast

## STRAWBERRY FILLING
1 qt. fresh strawberries
3 eggs
½ cup sugar
½ cup heavy cream

Make dough on the dough/manual cycle of the bread machine. Wash, hull and slice strawberries and set aside. Upon completion of the dough cycle, remove dough from the machine, roll it into a 9-x-13-inch rectangle and place it in a buttered 9-x-13-inch baking dish. Cover dough with strawberries. With a blender or electric mixer, beat eggs with sugar until sugar is dissolved. Mix in cream and pour custard mixture over fruit. Bake in a preheated 400° oven for 10 minutes; reduce heat to 350° and bake until custard is set, about 25 to 30 minutes. Serve warm or cold.

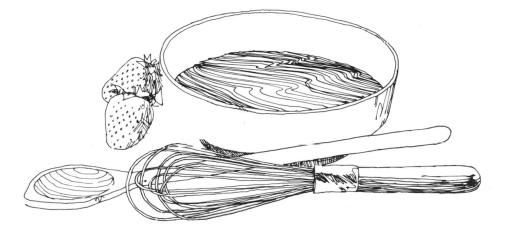

# WHITE CHOCOLATE YEAST CAKE

Servings: 8

*Yeast cakes are best made using the dough cycle of the machine because they generally require much longer rising times than the machines allow. I much prefer macadamia nuts in this recipe, but they are expensive and may be difficult to find. Almonds are a good substitute. The chips and nuts can be added at the beep if you have one on your machine, or after the dough has formed a smooth round ball; however, the chips will disappear into the dough. Since I prefer chunks of white chocolate, I knead them in by hand after the dough is removed from the machine.*

## DOUGH

¾ cup milk
4 oz. cream cheese, softened
2 tbs. butter or margarine
1 egg
1 tsp. vanilla extract

¼ cup sugar
1 tsp. salt
3 cups all-purpose flour
2 tsp. yeast

## ADDITIONS

½ cup white chocolate chips
½ cup macadamia nuts, finely chopped, or ½ cup sliced almonds

## WASH

1 egg beaten with 1-2 tbs. water, or cream only

Make dough on the dough/manual cycle of the bread machine. Upon completion of the dough cycle, place dough on a lightly floured surface and knead chocolate and nuts into dough. Shape dough into an approximate 8-inch round and place in a greased 9-inch round baking dish; it will spread into the baking dish as it rises. Cover with a towel and let rise until doubled in bulk, about 1½ hours. Brush with egg wash or cream and bake in a preheated 350° oven for 35 to 40 minutes, or until golden brown and the bottom sounds hollow when tapped.

# DRIED CHERRY YEAST CAKE

Servings: 8

*Dried cherries can be expensive, but are worth it in treats like this. If you really want to splurge, you can double the amount of the cherries.*

## DOUGH
½ cup milk
½ cup ricotta cheese
2 tbs. butter or margarine
1 egg
2 tsp. vanilla extract
¼ cup sugar
1 tsp. salt
3 cups all-purpose flour
2 tsp. yeast

## ADDITION
½ cup dried cherries

## WASH
1 egg, beaten with 1-2 tbs. water, or cream only

Make dough on the dough/manual cycle of the bread machine. Upon completion of the dough cycle, roll dough into a large rectangle on a lightly floured surface. Spread cherries evenly over dough and roll dough jelly roll-fashion from the long edge. Pinch ends together to make a circle, place in a greased Bundt pan or tube pan, cover with a towel and let rise until doubled in bulk, about 1½ hours. Brush with egg wash or cream and bake in a preheated 350° oven for 25 to 30 minutes until golden brown. Drizzle with *Glaze* if desired.

## GLAZE (OPTIONAL)
½ cup confectioners' sugar
2 tsp. vanilla or cherry extract
3-4 tbs. milk or cream

Mix glaze ingredients together, adding milk or cream until desired consistency is obtained. Drizzle over cake while still warm.

# FILLED BRIOCHE WREATH

Servings: 16

*This wreath makes a fancy breakfast or brunch presentation or a great holiday gift. I love watching people's reactions when they discover that the rolls are filled!*

## DOUGH
¾ cup milk
¼ cup butter
2 eggs
2 tbs. sugar
1 tsp. salt
3 cups all-purpose flour
2 tsp. yeast

## FILLING SUGGESTIONS
chocolate kisses or similar-sized chocolate pieces
lemon curd
any favorite preserve

1 tbs. butter, melted, for brushing

Make dough on the dough/manual cycle of the bread machine. Upon completion of the dough cycle, lightly flour your hands and the work surface to prevent sticking. Remove dough from machine and form into 16 equal balls. Press each ball between the palms of your hands to flatten. Place a chocolate piece or a spoonful of lemon curd or preserves in the center of each piece of dough and pull sides of dough around filling to encase it, pinching with your fingers to seal tightly. Roll dough ball in melted butter. Place balls around the perimeter of a pizza pan (disposable if you are giving the wreath as a gift). Cover and let rise for about 30 minutes. Bake in a preheated 350° oven for 20 minutes or until golden brown.

# COLONIAL AMERICAN FRUIT DESSERT

Servings: 8

*Early Americans used every piece of bread, wasting nothing. This recipe is based on an early American fruit pudding.*

1 qt. blueberries, or 1 pkg. (16 oz.) frozen blueberries, thawed
1/2-3/4 cup sugar
1/4 cup water
7-8 slices *Fruit Bread*, page 15, *Lemon Bread*,
    page 16, or *Orange Bread*, page 17
1-2 tbs. butter, melted
whipped cream

Wash and clean fresh berries. In a large saucepan, heat berries with 1/2 cup sugar and the water. Bring to a boil, stirring frequently, until berries are soft. Add more sugar if necessary, to taste. Remove from heat and set aside. Remove crusts from bread. Brush one side of each slice of bread with melted butter. Press 1/2 of the bread (buttered side up) into a greased 8-inch round (or square) baking dish. Pour hot berries on top and cover with remaining bread (buttered side up), so that berries are completely covered. Cover with aluminum foil and weigh down with a plate. Refrigerate for 6 to 8 hours or overnight. Serve with whipped cream.

# INDEX

# SERVE CREATIVE, EASY, NUTRITIOUS MEALS WITH nitty gritty® COOKBOOKS

Edible Pockets for Every Meal
Cooking With Chile Peppers
Oven and Rotisserie Roasting
Risottos, Paellas and Other Rice
 Specialties
Entrées From Your Bread Machine
Muffins, Nut Breads and More
Healthy Snacks for Kids
100 Dynamite Desserts
Recipes for Yogurt Cheese
Sautés
Cooking in Porcelain
Appetizers
Casseroles
The Best Bagels are made at home*
 (*perfect for your bread machine)
The Toaster Oven Cookbook
Skewer Cooking on the Grill
Creative Mexican Cooking
Extra-Special Crockery Pot Recipes
Slow Cooking
Cooking in Clay
Marinades
Deep Fried Indulgences

Cooking with Parchment Paper
The Garlic Cookbook
From Your Ice Cream Maker
Cappuccino/Espresso: The Book of
 Beverages
The Best Pizza is made at home*
 (*perfect for your bread machine)
The Well Dressed Potato
Convection Oven Cookery
The Steamer Cookbook
The Pasta Machine Cookbook
The Versatile Rice Cooker
The Dehydrator Cookbook
The Bread Machine Cookbook
The Bread Machine Cookbook II
The Bread Machine Cookbook III
The Bread Machine Cookbook IV:
 *Whole Grains and Natural Sugars*
The Bread Machine Cookbook V:
 *Favorite Recipes from 100 Kitchens*
The Bread Machine Cookbook VI:
 *Hand-Shaped Breads from the
 Dough Cycle*

Worldwide Sourdoughs From Your
 Bread Machine
Recipes for the Pressure Cooker
The New Blender Book
The Sandwich Maker Cookbook
Waffles
Indoor Grilling
The Coffee Book
The Juicer Books I and II
Bread Baking (traditional)
No Salt, No Sugar, No Fat Cookbook
Cooking for 1 or 2
Quick and Easy Pasta Recipes
The 9x13 Pan Cookbook
Recipes for the Loaf Pan
Low Fat American Favorites
Now That's Italian!
Healthy Cooking on the Run
The Wok
Favorite Seafood Recipes
New International Fondue Cookbook
Favorite Cookie Recipes
Flatbreads From Around the World

For a free catalog, write or call:
Bristol Publishing Enterprises, Inc.
P.O. Box 1737, San Leandro, CA 94577
(800) 346-4889; in California, (510) 895-4461